GRADE **1**

t s

# Review

**Quick Tip**

Numbers in words:

| 1 | 2 | 3 | 4 | 5 | 6 | 7 | 8 | 9 | 10 |
|---|---|---|---|---|---|---|---|---|----|
| one | two | three | four | five | six | seven | eight | nine | ten |

Some words telling the order of things:

| 1st | 2nd | 3rd | 4th | 5th | 6th | 7th | 8th | 9th | 10th |
|-----|-----|-----|-----|-----|-----|-----|-----|-----|------|
| first | second | third | fourth | fifth | sixth | seventh | eighth | ninth | tenth |

## Count and write the numbers in the boxes. Then write the numbers in words.

① ② ③ ④

## Look at the aliens and fill in the blanks.

Sam   Wilson   Alex   Tim   Lucy   Eric   Paul   George

⑤ _____ is the 3rd and _____ is the 7th on the line.

⑥ Lucy is the _____ and George is the _____ on the line.

⑦ There are _____ aliens on the line.

## *What comes next?* *Colour the correct picture for each group.*

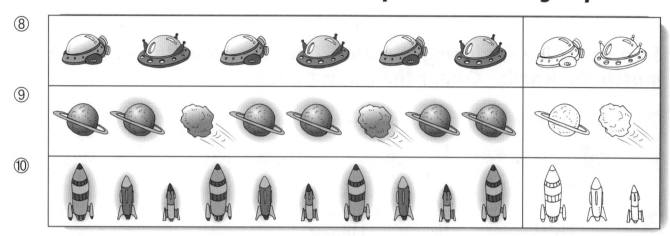

⑧
⑨
⑩

## *Fill in the missing numbers in each group.*

⑪ 1   2   ☐   4   ☐   ☐

⑫ 4   5   ☐   ☐   8   ☐

⑬ ☐   6   7   ☐   9   ☐

## Circle the correct words.

⑭ Sam the alien is   inside / outside   the
🛸 .

⑮ Sam the alien is   behind / in front of
the 🪐 .

⑯ Sam the alien is   above / below   the
🪐 .

⑰ Sam the alien is wearing a 🔘   on / in
its head.

**Sam the alien is visiting a farm. Help him find the objects that match the words. Colour the correct ones.**

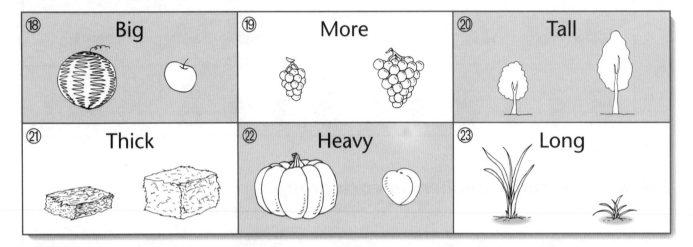

⑱ Big

⑲ More

⑳ Tall

㉑ Thick

㉒ Heavy

㉓ Long

**Help Sam the alien put the pictures in order. Write the letters.**

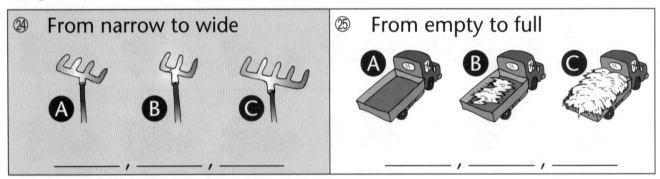

㉔ From narrow to wide

A    B    C

_____ , _____ , _____

㉕ From empty to full

A    B    C

_____ , _____ , _____

**Sort the objects in each group. Cross out ✗ the one that does not belong.**

㉖

㉗

㉘

㉙

## *Join the matching solids with lines for Sam.*

㉚

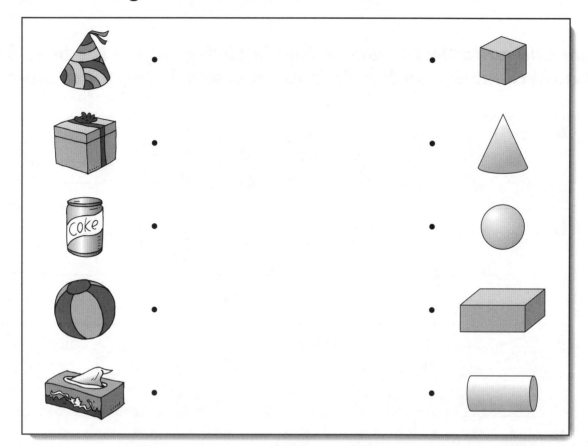

## *Help Sam the alien trace and colour the shapes. Then colour the shapes in the picture with the same colours used for colouring the shapes in ㉛.*

㉛

| Rectangle - blue | Triangle - green | Circle - yellow | Square - red |
|---|---|---|---|

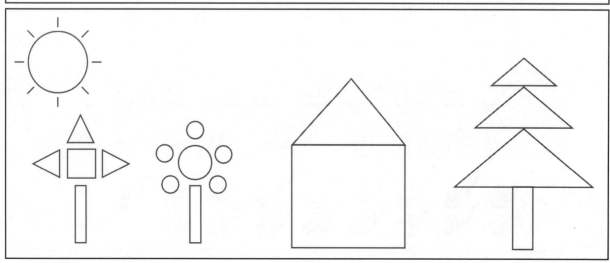

㉜

# 1 Numbers 1 - 20

Count and write the number of toys in each group in the box. Then put a check mark ✔ in the circle to show which group has more.

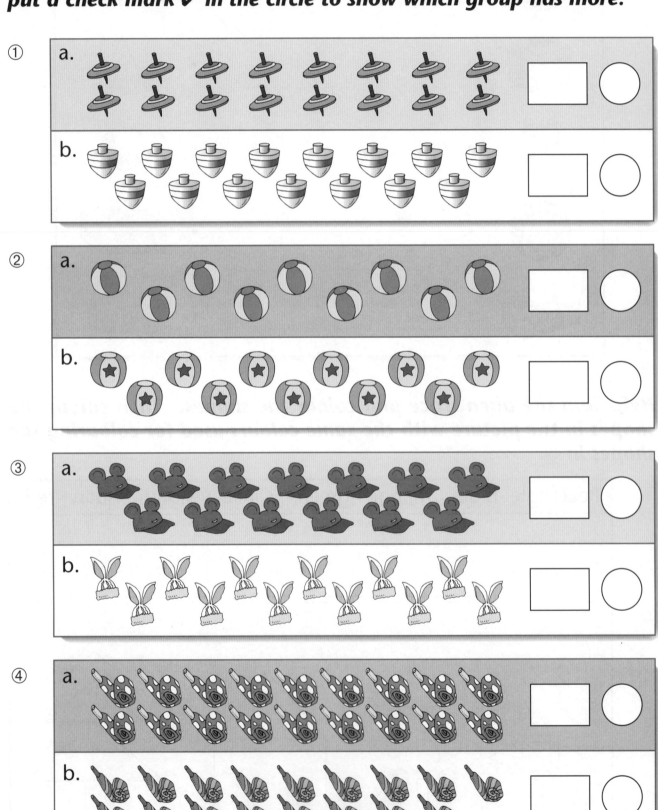

## Count the toys.  Then write the numbers in the boxes.

| | | | | | |
|---|---|---|---|---|---|
| ⑤ | | ⑥ | | ⑦ | |
| ⑧ | | ⑨ | | ⑩ | |

## Circle the correct words.

⑪ Eleven / Thirteen  is one more than twelve.

⑫ Seventeen is one less than  sixteen / eighteen .

⑬ Eighteen / Fourteen  is two more than sixteen.

⑭ Thirteen is  one / two / three  less than fifteen.

⑮ Twenty is  one / two / three  more than nineteen.

| | |
|---|---|
| eleven | 11 |
| twelve | 12 |
| thirteen | 13 |
| fourteen | 14 |
| fifteen | 15 |
| sixteen | 16 |
| seventeen | 17 |
| eighteen | 18 |
| nineteen | 19 |
| twenty | 20 |

## Add picture(s) to each group to match the number in the circle.

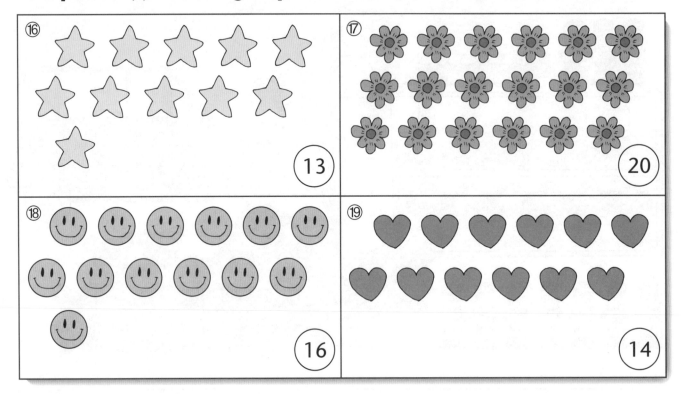

## Cross out X picture(s) in each group to match the number in the circle.

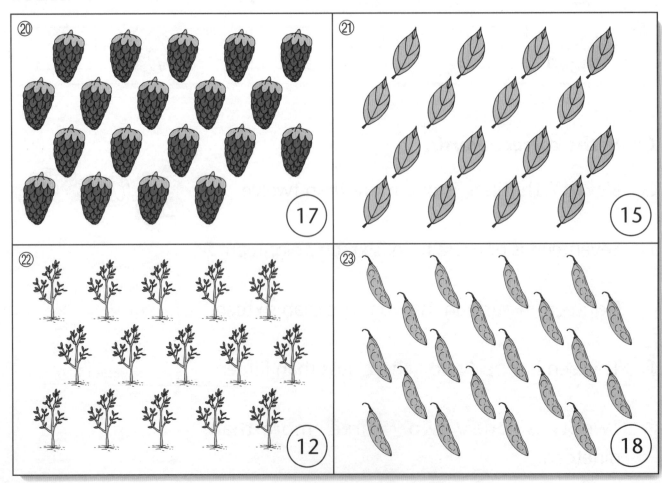

## Look at the pictures.  Write the numbers.

㉔

There are _____ bears in all ; _____ 🐻 and _____ 🐻 .

㉕

There are _____ fish in all ; _____ 🐟 and _____ 🐟 .

㉖

There are _____ dogs in all ; _____ 🐕 and _____ 🐕 .

## Count how many butterflies are in each group.  Then fill in the blanks.

㉗ There are _____ 🦋 in the 1st group and _____ 🦋 in the 2nd group.

㉘ There is/are _____ 🦋 more in the 2nd group than the 1st group.

 **MIND BOGGLER**

**Read what Tim says.  Draw and colour the apples to find out how many apples Tim has.**

I have 4 red apples, 2 green apples and 3 golden apples.

Tim has _____ apples in all.

# Sequencing

**Put the pictures in order.  Write the numbers 1 - 4 in the boxes.**

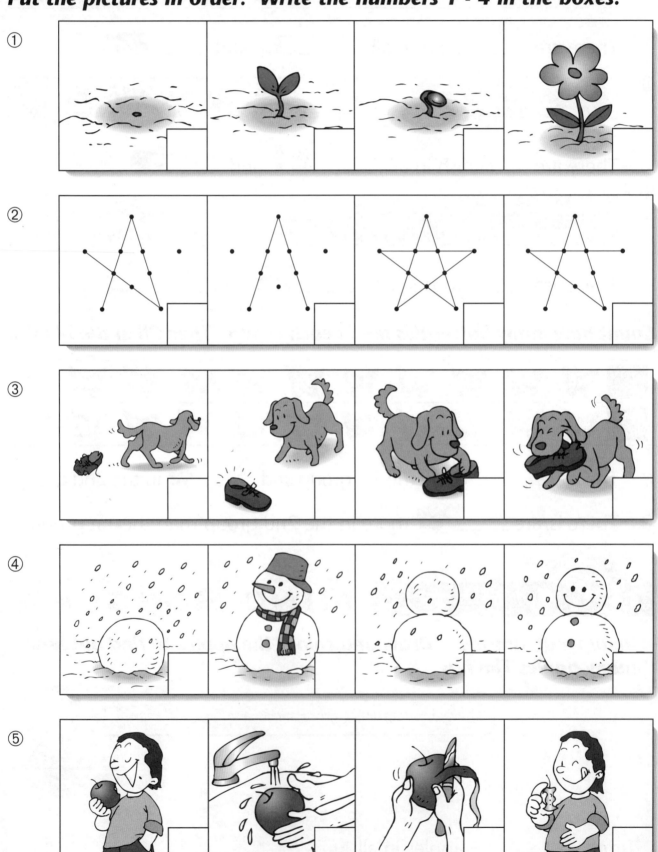

## Look at the patterns. Draw the missing shapes in the blanks.

⑥

⑦

⑧

⑨

## Draw the patterns.

⑩ Use 3 circles to make 2 more patterns which are different from the one below.

⑪ Use 4 squares to make 2 more patterns which are different from the one below.

⑫ Use 1 square and 2 triangles to make 2 more patterns which are different from the one below.

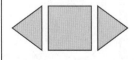

## Complete the patterns.

⑬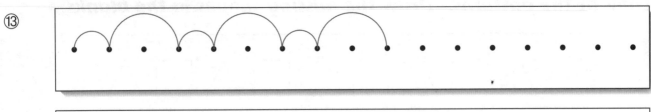

⑭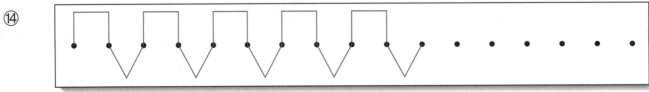

⑮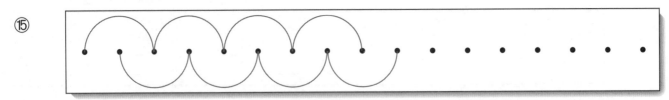

## Which one is the missing picture for each pattern?  Colour it.

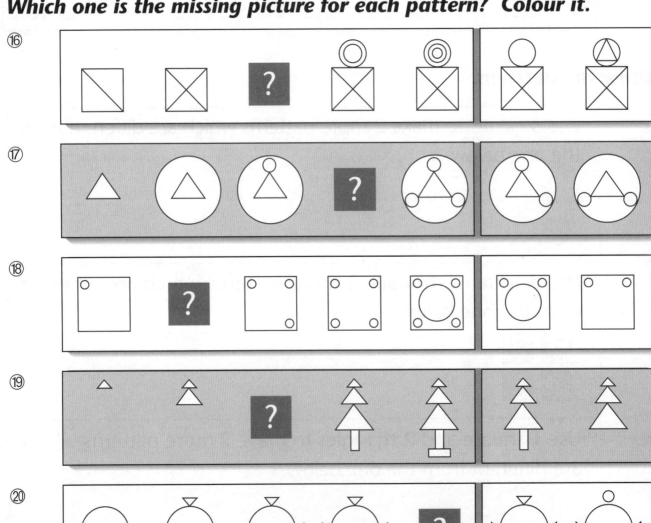

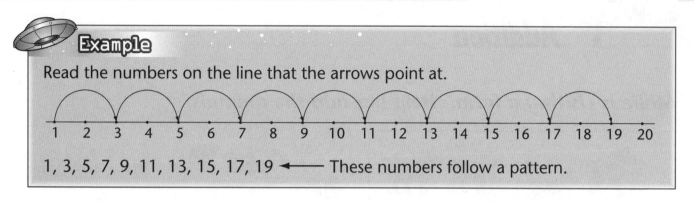

**Example**

Read the numbers on the line that the arrows point at.

1, 3, 5, 7, 9, 11, 13, 15, 17, 19 ◀——— These numbers follow a pattern.

## Fill in the missing numbers on the trains.

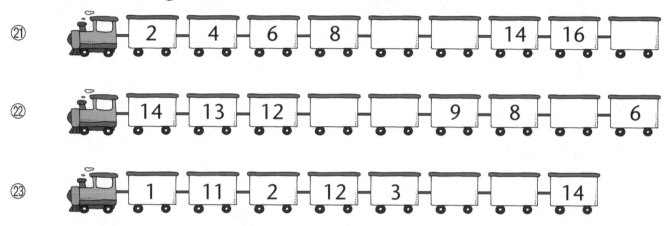

㉑ 2 — 4 — 6 — 8 — ☐ — ☐ — 14 — 16 — ☐

㉒ 14 — 13 — 12 — ☐ — ☐ — 9 — 8 — ☐ — 6

㉓ 1 — 11 — 2 — 12 — 3 — ☐ — ☐ — 14

## Fill in the missing numbers.

| ㉔ | 1 | 2 | 3 | 1 |  | 3 | 1 | 2 |  | 1 |

| ㉕ | 7 | 8 | 10 | 7 | 8 |  | 7 |  | 10 |

| ㉖ | 10 | 10 | 9 | 10 | 10 |  | 10 |  | 9 | 10 |  | 9 |

**MIND BOGGLER**

### Draw the next 2 pictures for the pattern below.

    _____ _____

# 3 Addition

## Millie is visiting a farm.  Help her add the animals.

①

3 + 4 = _____

*Quick Tip*

We can use addition to find out how many things there are in all,

e.g. 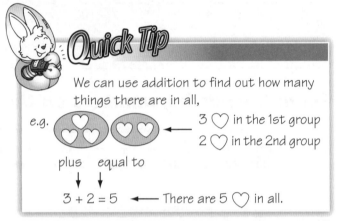 ← 3 ♡ in the 1st group
2 ♡ in the 2nd group

plus    equal to
↓        ↓
3 + 2 = 5  ← There are 5 ♡ in all.

②

5 + 1 = _____

③

4 + 4 = _____

④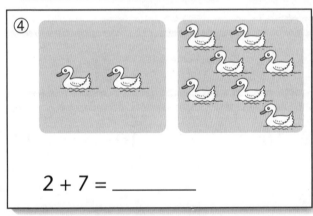

2 + 7 = _____

⑤

3 + 5 = _____

⑥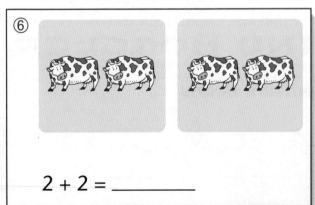

2 + 2 = _____

⑦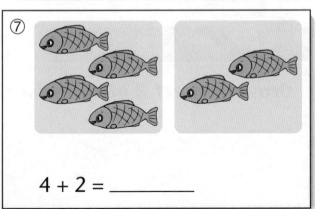

4 + 2 = _____

## Use the cubes to help you find the answers.

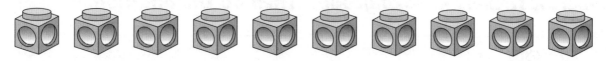

⑧ 2 + 4 = _____    ⑨ 3 + 5 = _____    ⑩ 3 + 2 = _____

⑪ 4 + 5 = _____    ⑫ 6 + 2 = _____    ⑬ 4 + 3 = _____

⑭ 1 + 5 = _____    ⑮ 3 + 7 = _____    ⑯ 2 + 8 = _____

⑰ 5 + 5 = _____

⑱ 6 + 3 = _____

⑲ 4 + 4 = _____

> "+" means ADD. It also means "Join the groups to find the total."
>
> e.g.    2 + 3 = _____
>
>            1st group      2nd group
>
>
>
>         1   2     3   4   5 ← Keep counting to find the total.
>
> 2 + 3 = __5__

## Complete the addition table.

⑳

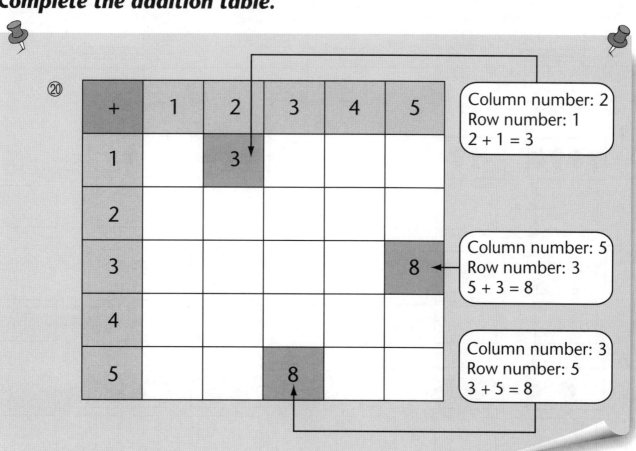

| + | 1 | 2 | 3 | 4 | 5 |
|---|---|---|---|---|---|
| 1 |  | 3 |  |  |  |
| 2 |  |  |  |  |  |
| 3 |  |  |  |  | 8 |
| 4 |  |  |  |  |  |
| 5 |  |  | 8 |  |  |

Column number: 2
Row number: 1
2 + 1 = 3

Column number: 5
Row number: 3
5 + 3 = 8

Column number: 3
Row number: 5
3 + 5 = 8

**See how Nancy puts her stickers into groups. Count and write the number of stickers in each group. Then do the addition.**

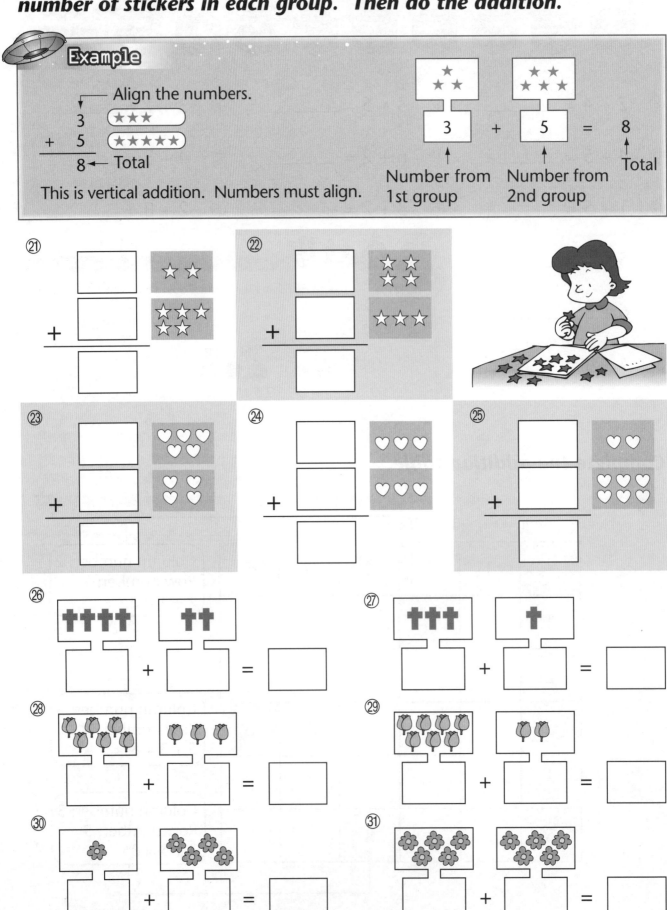

**Andy and his friends are going fishing. Look at the fish they catch.**
**Read the sentences and add the fish. Then write the children's names.**

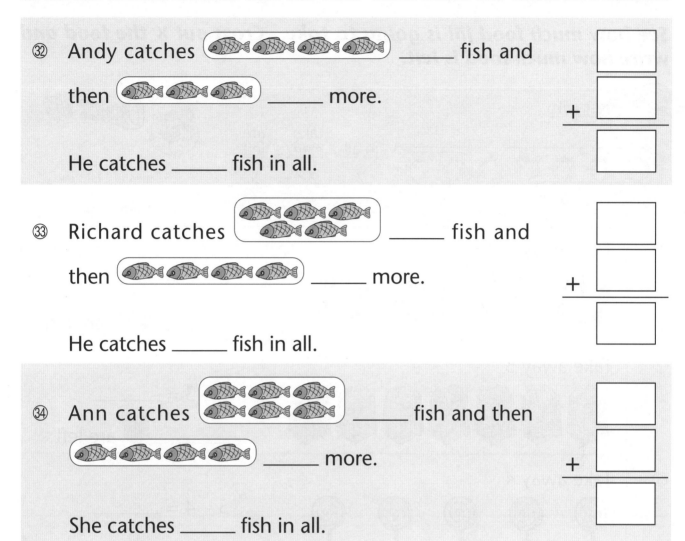

③② Andy catches _____ _____ fish and

then _____ _____ more.

He catches _____ fish in all.

③③ Richard catches _____ _____ fish and

then _____ _____ more.

He catches _____ fish in all.

③④ Ann catches _____ _____ fish and then

_____ _____ more.

She catches _____ fish in all.

③⑤ _____ catches the most fish.

③⑥ _____ catches the fewest fish.

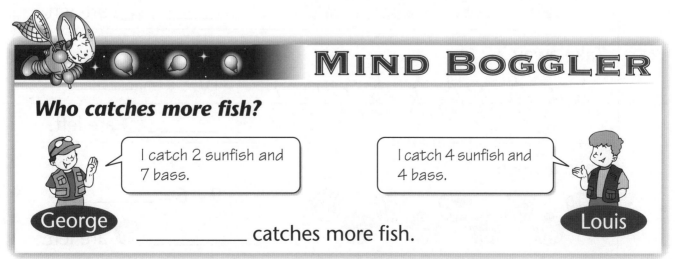

# MIND BOGGLER

**Who catches more fish?**

I catch 2 sunfish and 7 bass.

I catch 4 sunfish and 4 bass.

George

Louis

_____ catches more fish.

# 4 Subtraction

**See how much food Jill is going to take. Cross out ✗ the food and write how much food is left.**

**Quick Tip**

" – " means " Take away ".

### Example

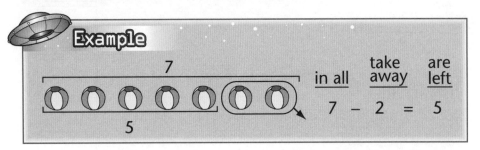

| | in all | take away | are left |
|---|---|---|---|
| 7 | 7 – | 2 = | 5 |

5

---

① Take away 2

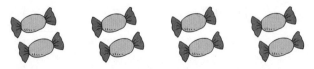

8 – 2 = _____

_____  are left.

---

② Take away 3

7 – 3 = _____

_____ are left.

---

③ Take away 4

5 – 4 = _____

_____ is left.

---

④ Take away 3

8 – 3 = _____

_____ are left.

---

⑤ Take away 2

10 – 2 = _____

_____ are left.

---

⑥ Take away 6

9 – 6 = _____

_____ are left.

## Write how many shapes are crossed out and find the answers.

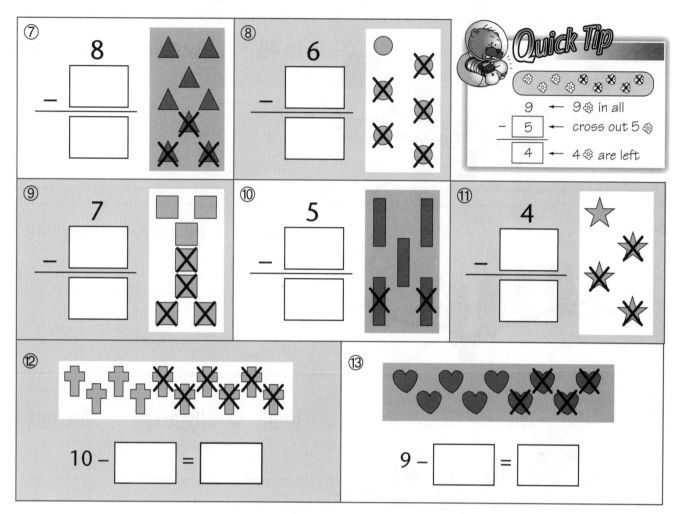

## Use the building blocks to help you find the answers.

⑭
$$8$$
$$- \ 3$$

⑮
$$5$$
$$- \ 2$$

⑯
$$4$$
$$- \ 1$$

⑰
$$6$$
$$- \ 4$$

⑱ 9 – 3 = _____

⑲ 5 – 4 = _____

⑳ 10 – 2 = _____

㉑ 7 – 5 = _____

㉒ 6 – 3 = _____

㉓ 9 – 2 = _____

㉔ 8 – 4 = _____

㉕ 6 – 2 = _____

# Look at the birds.  See how many birds fly away.  Write the numbers.

㉖

<u>in all</u>      <u>fly away</u>      <u>are left</u>

_____ – _____ = _____

㉗

<u>in all</u>      <u>fly away</u>      <u>are left</u>

_____ – _____ = _____

㉘

<u>in all</u>      <u>fly away</u>      <u>are left</u>

_____ – _____ = _____

㉙

<u>in all</u>      <u>fly away</u>      <u>are left</u>

_____ – _____ = _____

㉚

<u>in all</u>      <u>fly away</u>      <u>are left</u>

_____ – _____ =

***Read what Tommy Turtle says. Write the numbers.***

㉛ I collect 5 seashells. I give 2 seashells to my friend. Now I have ☐ seashells.

㉜ There are 6 crabs on the beach. 3 crabs crawl back to the sea. Now there are ☐ crabs on the beach.

㉝ There are 9 fish. 2 fish are big and ☐ fish are small.

㉞ There are 8 rocks. I take away 5 rocks. ☐ rocks are left.

㉟ I see 7 shrimps. 5 shrimps swim away. ☐ shrimps are left.

㊱ I see 4 starfish. 2 starfish swim away. ☐ starfish are left.

㊲ There are 10 frogs. 4 frogs go swimming. ☐ frogs are still on the bank.

㊳ There are 9 seals. 3 seals lie on the rocks. ☐ seals go swimming.

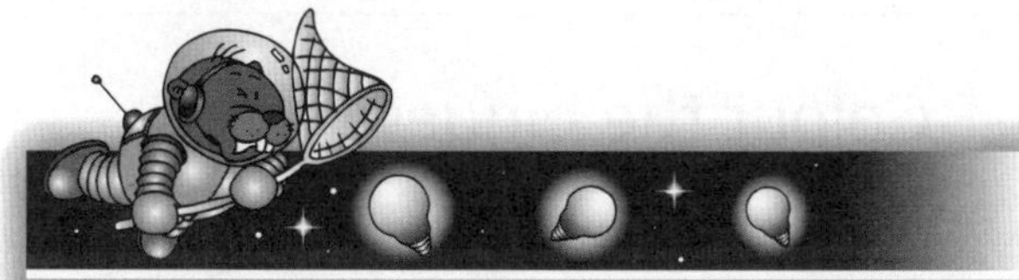

## MIND BOGGLER

***Sabrina Turtle has 10 shells to make three necklaces. She has made 2 necklaces. How many shells are left for the third necklace?***

______ shells are left for the third necklace.

# 5 Measurement I

## Colour the correct pictures.

① Colour the tallest.

② Colour the widest.

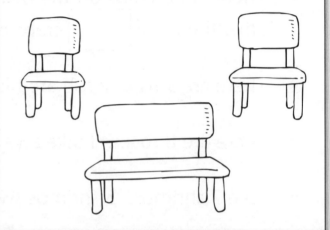

③ Colour the heaviest.

④ Colour the longest.

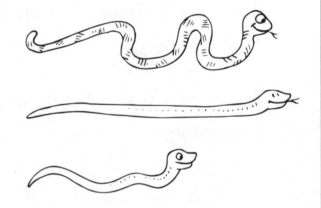

⑤ Colour the thinnest.

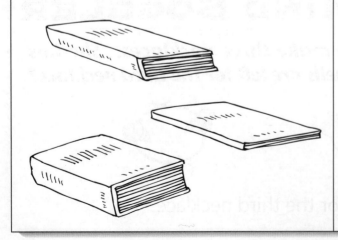

⑥ Colour the biggest.

**Dolly is measuring her things.  See about how many thumbs and paper clips she uses to measure them.  Write the numbers.**

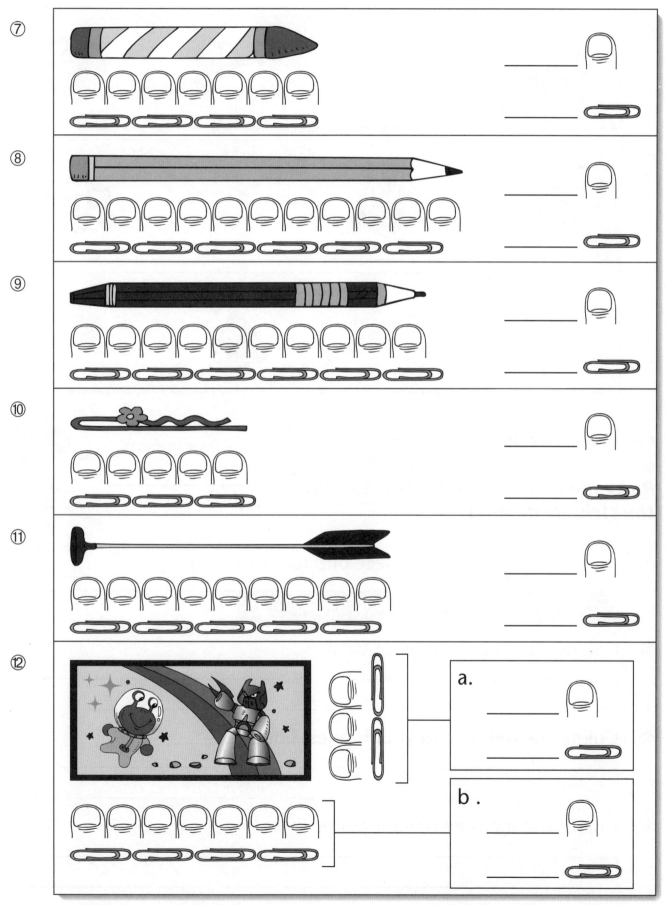

**Ricky wants to measure the things with his toys. Which is the best unit for measuring each thing? Put a check mark ✔ in the circles.**

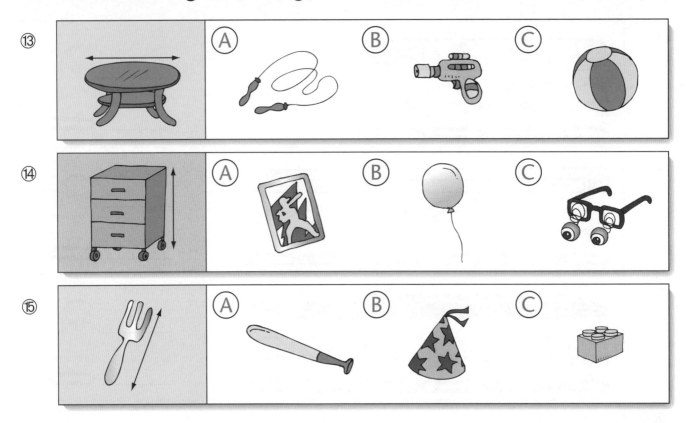

⑬ (A) (B) (C)

⑭ (A) (B) (C)

⑮ (A) (B) (C)

**Cut a strip of paper the same length as the one shown below. See how Ricky measures his wrist and colour the strip as he does.**

This is the measure of my wrist.

| Cut a piece of paper this long |
|---|

| Measure of Ricky's wrist | |
|---|---|

⑯ Colour the measure of your wrist.

| |
|---|

⑰ Colour the measure of your longest finger.

| |
|---|

⑱ Colour the measure of your palm.

| |
|---|

**Ricky has cards of different shapes. See how he uses pennies to cover one of the cards. Then follow his way to measure the cards below.**

I use 6 pennies to cover this card.

⑲ **A**

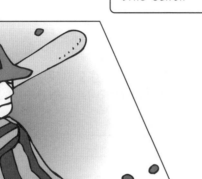

**B**

**C**  **D**

A : _____ pennies

B : _____ pennies

C : _____ pennies

D : _____ pennies

# MIND BOGGLER

**Uncle Bill drops some paint on the floor by accident. See how many squares that the paint covers. Write the number.**

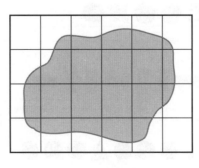

*Quick Tip*

Combine the partly covered squares to form a square.

The paint covers about _____ squares.

# 6 Patterns

**Look at these sets. Check ✔ the one that is a pattern. Otherwise, put a cross ✗ in the circle.**

**Examples**

① Is ABABABABAB a pattern?
AB repeats itself.
ABABABABAB is a pattern.

② Is 13452314 a pattern?
No, it is not a pattern.

**Quick Tip**

A pattern is a way in which something happens again and again.

① A B B A B B A B B A B B A B B A B B  ◯

② ▲ ■ ● ● ▲ ■ ● ● ▲ ■ ● ● ▲ ■ ● ●  ◯

③ 1 2 3 3 1 1 2 3 1 3 2 1 3 1 2 2 3 1 1 2 3 1  ◯

④ $ $ ¢ ¢ $ ¢ $ ¢ ¢ $ $ ¢ ¢ $ $ ¢ $ ¢ $ $  ◯

**Find the group of shapes repeating in each pattern. Write the number of shapes in each group. Then draw the shapes out.**

⑤ ◆ ▲ ▲ ◆ ▲ ▲ ◆ ◆ ▲ ▲ ◆ ▲ ▲   _____ ; _____

⑥ ★ ★ ♥ ♥ ★ ★ ♥ ♥ ★ ★ ♥ ♥ ★ ★ ♥ ♥   _____ ; _____

⑦ ● ■ ● ● ■ ● ● ■ ● ● ■ ●   _____ ; _____

⑧ ❚❚ ▬ ❚❚ ▬ ❚❚ ▬ ❚❚ ▬ ❚❚ ▬   _____ ; _____

⑨ ▲ ● ● ● ▲ ● ● ● ▲ ● ● ● ▲ ● ● ●   _____ ; _____

26

## Extend the patterns.

⑩    ✕   ◯   ✕   ◯   ✕   ◯   ✕   ◯   ✕    _____   _____   _____

⑪    **4   4   6   3   4   4   6   3   4**    _____   _____   _____

⑫    **G   T   P   G   G   T   P   G   G**    _____   _____   _____

⑬    ◯   ○   ∘   ◯   ○   ∘   ◯   ○   ∘    _____   _____   _____

⑭    △   ▲   ▽   △   ▲   ▽   △   ▲   ▽    _____   _____   _____

## Ben and Bill are painting a pattern.  Help them choose the shapes from the pattern code and colour the shapes.

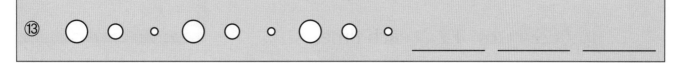

1 = yellow △     2 = red ◯     3 = blue ☐

4 = green ☐     5 = purple ⬡

⑮    _____   _____   _____   _____   _____   _____   _____   _____
      1      2      2      3      1      2      2      3

⑯    _____   _____   _____   _____   _____   _____   _____   _____
      4      2      5      4      2      5      4      2

⑰    _____   _____   _____   _____   _____   _____   _____   _____
      4      3      3      1      4      3      3      1

⑱    _____   _____   _____   _____   _____   _____   _____   _____
      5      2      4      3      5      2      4      3

**Write the number of shaded triangles in each picture and follow the pattern to draw and shade the next picture. Then circle the correct answers.**

⑲ a.

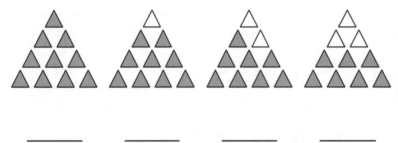

b.

_____  _____  _____  _____

c. The number of shaded triangles goes

   up / down  by  1 / 2  each time.

⑳ a.

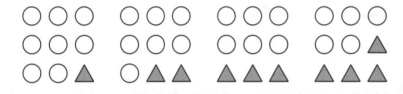

b.

_____  _____  _____  _____

c. The number of  circles / triangles  goes

   up by  1 / 2  each time.

**Look at the two magic washing machines. After washing the clothes, how do the numbers on the clothes change? Write the new numbers.**

㉑

㉒

# Cross out **X** one of the pictures in each set so that it follows a pattern.

㉓

㉔

㉕

# Colour the hearts and answer the questions.

㉖ a. For the 1st row, colour the 1st, 4th and 7th hearts green and the rest blue.

b. For the 2nd row, colour the 2nd, 5th and 8th hearts green and the rest blue.

c. For the 3rd row, colour the 3rd and 6th hearts green and the rest blue.

| 1st row | ♡ ♡ ♡ ♡ ♡ ♡ ♡ ♡ |
| 2nd row | ♡ ♡ ♡ ♡ ♡ ♡ ♡ ♡ |
| 3rd row | ♡ ♡ ♡ ♡ ♡ ♡ ♡ ♡ |

d. Do the rows have a pattern?  _____

 **MIND BOGGLER**

**Which 2 attributes do the figures have?  Write 'pattern', 'shape' or 'size' to fill in the blanks.**

①

②

All the figures have the same            All the figures have the same

_____ and _____ .            _____ and _____ .

# 7 2-D Figures

**Colour the shapes that look like the one on the left.**

① ② ③ ④

**Look at the shapes.   Check ✔ the correct description for each shape.**

⑤ 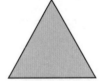   Ⓐ It has 3 sides.
Ⓑ It has 4 sides.

*Quick Tip*

To prevent from counting repeatedly, you can write the numbers beside the sides, e.g.

```
      2
   ┌──────┐
 1 │      │ 3    A square has 4 sides.
   └──────┘
      4
```

⑥    Ⓐ It has 5 sides.
Ⓑ It has 6 sides.

⑦

⑧

Ⓐ Its 4 sides are the same.

Ⓑ 2 of its sides are the same.

Ⓐ Its 4 sides are the same.

Ⓑ It has 4 sides.

# Write the names of the shapes. Then write the numbers.

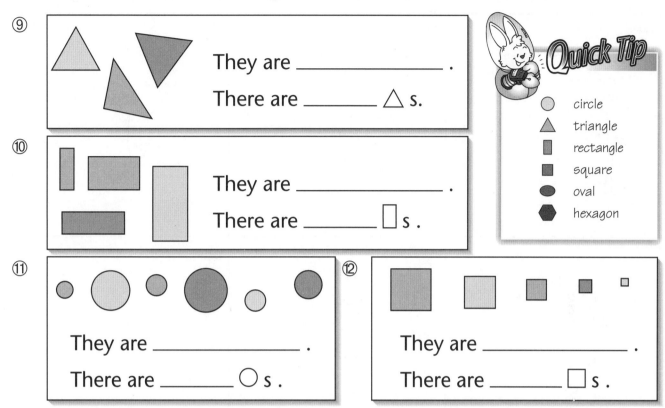

⑨

They are _____ .

There are _____ △ s.

⑩

They are _____ .

There are _____ □ s .

**Quick Tip**

⬭ circle
△ triangle
▯ rectangle
▪ square
⬭ oval
⬡ hexagon

⑪

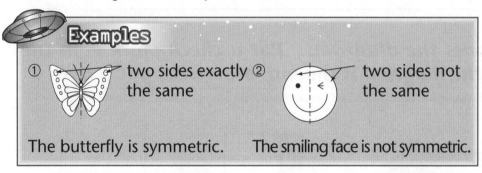

They are _____ .

There are _____ ○ s .

⑫

They are _____ .

There are _____ □ s .

# Are these pictures symmetric? Circle 'Yes' or 'No'.

**Examples**

① two sides exactly the same  ② two sides not the same

The butterfly is symmetric.  The smiling face is not symmetric.

**Quick Tip**

Symmetry means that 2 sides of a picture are exactly the same.

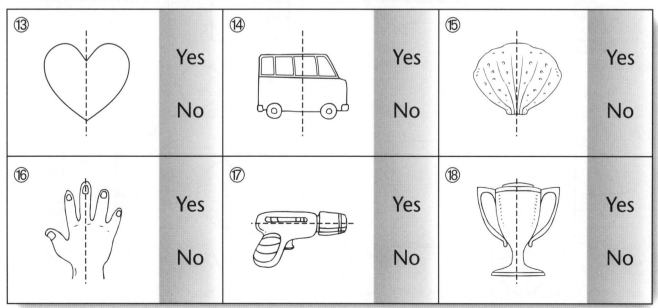

⑬ Yes  No

⑭ Yes  No

⑮ Yes  No

⑯ Yes  No

⑰ Yes  No

⑱ Yes  No

## Finish each picture to make it symmetric.

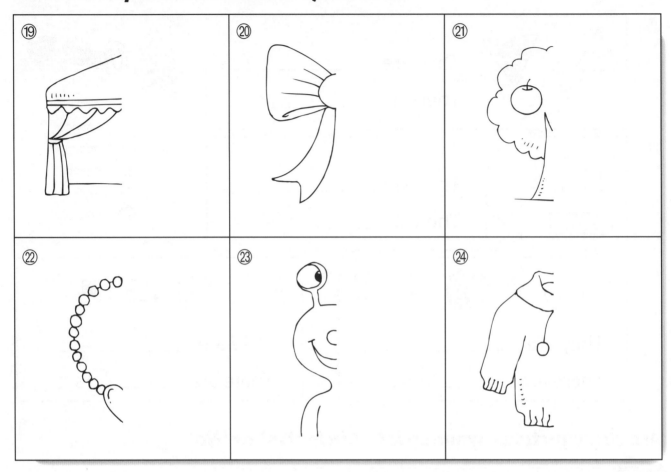

**See how Jimmy shades the diagrams. Put a check mark ✔ in the circle if one half of the diagram is shaded; otherwise, put a cross ✗.**

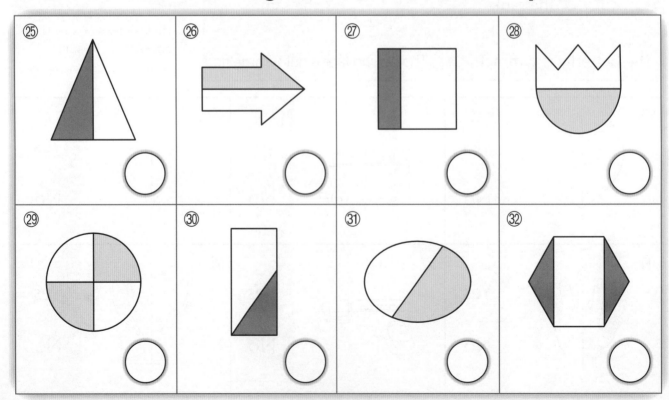

## Help Andy draw one shape on each piece of drawing paper on the board. Then answer the questions.

- ☜ An oval on the left and a rectangle on the right of the triangle
- ☜ A circle on the left of the oval
- ☜ A rectangle on the left and two circles on the right of the square
- ☜ A square under the rectangle
- ☜ A triangle on each side of the hexagon

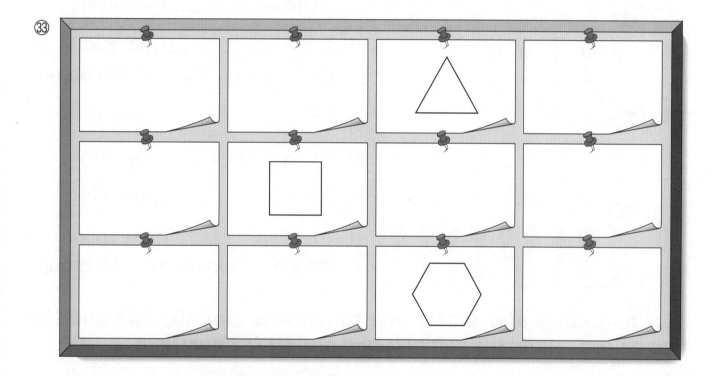

㉝

㉞ How many circles are there in all? _____

㉟ How many rectangles are there in all? _____

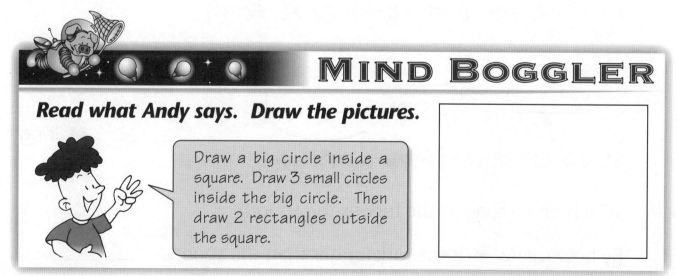

**MIND BOGGLER**

**Read what Andy says. Draw the pictures.**

Draw a big circle inside a square. Draw 3 small circles inside the big circle. Then draw 2 rectangles outside the square.

## Count the number of things for each group. Fill in the blanks.

①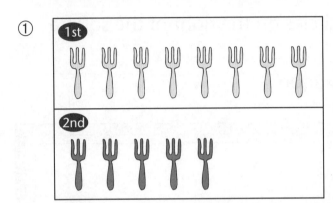

a. 1st group : _____ forks

b. 2nd group : _____ forks.

c. There are _____ forks in all.

d. There are _____ more forks in the 1st group than the 2nd group.

② 

a. 1st group : _____ spoons

b. 2nd group : _____ spoons

c. There are _____ spoons in all.

d. There are _____ more spoons in the 2nd group than the 1st group.

## See how many pins Shirley uses to tell how long the fork and the spoon are. Write the numbers and answer the questions.

③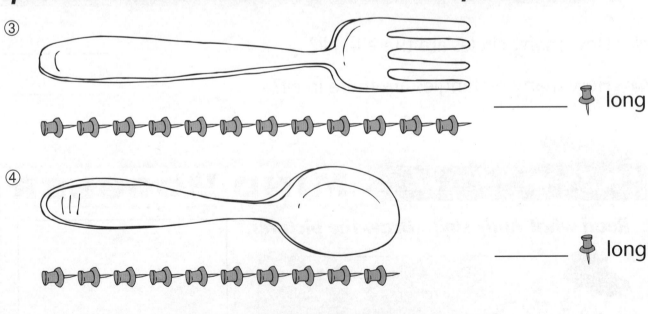

_____ 📌 long

④ 

_____ 📌 long

⑤ Which one is longer, the fork or the spoon?  _____

⑥ By how many 📌 is the fork longer than the spoon?  _____ 📌

34

## Put the pictures in order. Write the numbers 1 - 4 in the boxes.

## Do the addition or subtraction.

_____ + _____ = _____

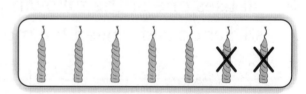

_____ + _____ = _____

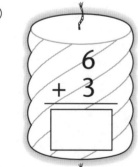

_____ – _____ = _____

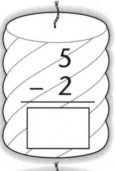

_____ – _____ = _____

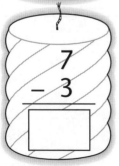

⑬ 6 + 3

⑭ 5 – 2

⑮ 8 – 4

⑯ 2 + 4

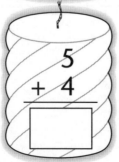

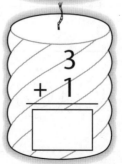

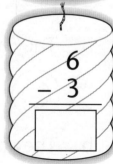

⑰ 7 – 3

⑱ 5 + 4

⑲ 3 + 1

⑳ 6 – 3

**Jill uses squares to measure the cards.  Help her count how many squares each card covers and check ✔ the correct answers.**

⟨21⟩  Card A : _____ squares          ⟨22⟩  Card B : _____ squares

⟨23⟩  Which card covers more squares?          Ⓐ Card A   Ⓑ Card B

⟨24⟩  Jill uses one of the following stickers to do measurement.  Which sticker does she need the most to cover Card A?

Ⓐ          Ⓑ          Ⓒ

**Extend the patterns and name the shapes.**

⟨25⟩  a.  △ ▲ △ ▲ △ ▲ ___ ___ ___ ___ ___

      b.  They are _____ .

⟨26⟩  a.  ☐ ☐ ☐ ☐ ☐ ☐ ___ ___ ___ ___ ___

      b.  They are _____ .

⟨27⟩  a.  ◎ ○ ○ ◎ ○ ○ ___ ___ ___ ___ ___

      b.  They are _____ .

# Write the numbers on the lines.  Then solve the problems.

㉘ Jill bought _____ 🎉 and _____ 🪀 .  How many toys did she buy in all?

_____ ( + ) _____ = _____

She bought _____ toys in all.

㉙ Jill had _____ 🎩 .  She gave 7 🎩 to her friends.  How many 🎩 does she have now?

_____ ( ) _____ = _____

She has _____ 🎩 now.

㉚ Jill's mom baked _____ 🍪 and _____ ⚫ .  How many cookies did she bake in all?

_____ ( ) _____ = _____

She baked _____ cookies in all.

㉛ There are _____ slices of pizza.  The children eat 9 slices.  How many slices are left?

_____ ( ) _____ = _____

_____ slice(s) is/are left.

㉜ Jill invited _____ friends to her party.  5 of them were boys.  How many were girls?

_____ ( ) _____ = _____

_____ were girls.

# 8  Numbers to 100

**Maxine Mouse is looking for a box of crackers that has exactly 42 crackers in it. Estimate how many crackers are in each box. Then circle every 10 crackers and count how many crackers are in each box. Answer the questions.**

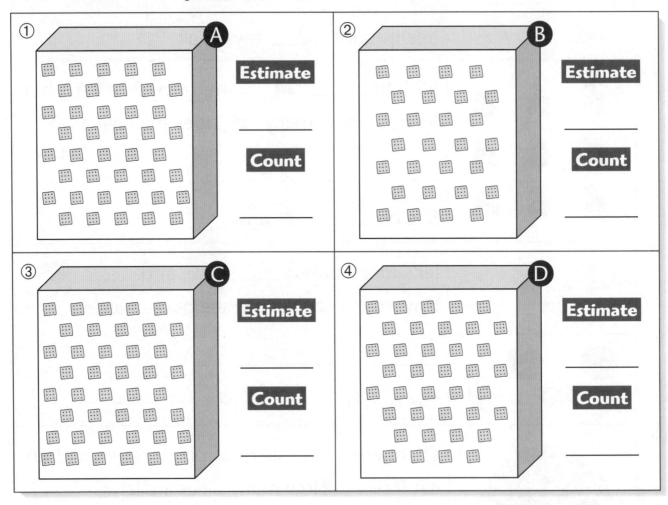

① **A**    Estimate _____    Count _____

② **B**    Estimate _____    Count _____

③ **C**    Estimate _____    Count _____

④ **D**    Estimate _____    Count _____

⑤ Which box of crackers is Maxine Mouse looking for?    Box _____

⑥ How many more crackers are in box C than in box A?    _____ cracker(s)

⑦ What is the difference between the number of crackers in box B and box D?    _____ cracker(s)

⑧ If Maxine Mouse takes 2 crackers from box C, how many crackers are still in box C?    _____ cracker(s)

Quick Tip

A fast way to count is to count by 10's.

e.g.   $\xrightarrow{+10}$ $\xrightarrow{+10}$ $\xrightarrow{+10}$
10 , 20 , 30 , 40 , ...

**The children are playing a card game. Read what Janice says. Help them complete the table and fill in the blanks.**

> Each of us gets 5 cards. Each round we have to take 1 card out. We compare our cards and the one with the biggest number wins the round.

⑨
⑩
⑪
⑫
⑬

| | Janice | Brenda | Lucy | Alex | Nancy | |
|---|---|---|---|---|---|---|
| 1st round | 25 | 19 | 42 | 35 | 40 | _____ wins. |
| 2nd round | 89 | 48 | 50 | 37 | 13 | _____ wins. |
| 3rd round | 40 | 22 | 31 | 60 | 15 | _____ wins. |
| 4th round | 70 | 65 | 82 | 41 | 20 | _____ wins. |
| 5th round | 53 | 26 | 48 | 10 | 88 | _____ wins. |

⑭ Who is the final winner in the 5 rounds? _____

⑮ Who never wins in the 5 rounds? _____

⑯ If Alex gets a [80] instead of [10] in the 5th round and

he deals this card, will he win that round? _____

⑰ Put the numbers in the 1st round in order from the biggest to the smallest.

[ ] , [ ] , [ ] , [ ] , [ ]

⑱ Put the numbers in the 4th round in order from the smallest to the biggest.

[ ] , [ ] , [ ] , [ ] , [ ]

39

# Count and write the number of building blocks in each group.

⑲

a. _____ tens and _____ ones     b. There are _____ 🧱 .

⑳

a. _____ tens and _____ ones     b. There are _____ 🧱 .

㉑

a. _____ tens and _____ ones     b. There are _____ 🧱 .

# Count the building blocks by 2's or 5's to see how many building blocks are in each group.

**Quick Tip**

Count by 2's: Number goes up by 2 each time.

e.g.  $2 \xrightarrow{+2} 4 \xrightarrow{+2} 6 \xrightarrow{+2} 8$

Count by 5's: Number goes up by 5 each time.

e.g.  $5 \xrightarrow{+5} 10 \xrightarrow{+5} 15 \xrightarrow{+5} 20$

㉒

㉓

㉔

㉕

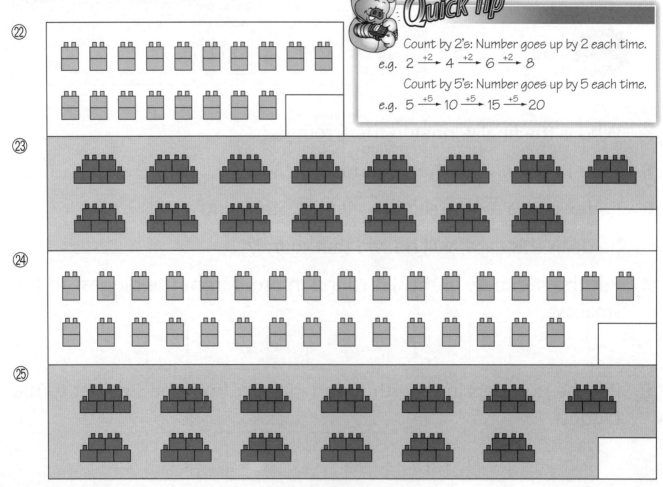

**Help the frogs jump to 50. Colour, circle or cross out ✘ the stones.**

㉖    Freddie frog jumps by 2's. Colour the stones in his route yellow.

㉗    Jenny frog jumps by 5's. Circle the stones in her route.

㉘    Lily frog jumps by 10's. Cross out ✘ the stones in her route.

# MIND BOGGLER

**Look at the questions ㉖ to ㉘. Answer the questions.**

①    Do Freddie and Jenny meet on ⟨15⟩ ?      _____

②    Do Jenny and Lily meet on ⟨35⟩ ?      _____

③    On which stones do Freddie and Lily meet?      _____

④    On which stones do the 3 frogs meet?      _____

# 9 Addition and Subtraction

**Sarah has bought some things for her birthday but she is going to buy more. Help her find out how many things she will have in all.**

| | Things Sarah bought | Things to be bought | |
|---|---|---|---|
| ① | | | 9 + 5 = _____ <br><br> _____ 🍔 in all |
| ② | | | _____ + _____ = _____ <br><br> _____ 🧃 in all |
| ③ | | | _____ + _____ = _____ <br><br> _____ 🎉 in all |
| ④ | | | _____ + _____ = _____ <br><br> _____ 🎈 in all |
| ⑤ | | | _____ + _____ = _____ <br><br> _____ 🧁 in all |
| ⑥ | | | _____ + _____ = _____ <br><br> _____ in all |

# Cross out X the exact amount of food to show how much food the children ate at Sarah's birthday party. Then find out how much food was left.

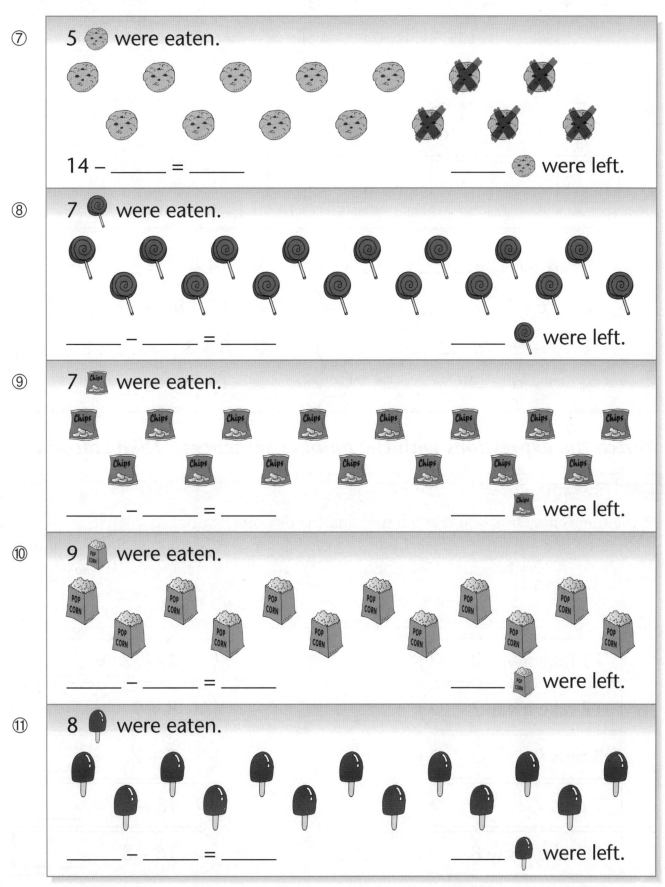

⑦ 5 🍪 were eaten.

14 – _____ = _____              _____ 🍪 were left.

⑧ 7 🍭 were eaten.

_____ – _____ = _____              _____ 🍭 were left.

⑨ 7 Chips were eaten.

_____ – _____ = _____              _____ Chips were left.

⑩ 9 POP CORN were eaten.

_____ – _____ = _____              _____ POP CORN were left.

⑪ 8 🍡 were eaten.

_____ – _____ = _____              _____ 🍡 were left.

## Add or subtract.

⑫
```
   1 2
 –   4
```
☐

⑬
```
     9
 +   8
```
☐

⑭
```
   1 5
 –   6
```
☐

⑮
```
     7
 +   8
```
☐

⑯
```
   1 1
 –   9
```
☐

⑰
```
     8
 +   5
```
☐

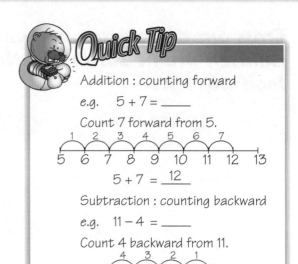

**Quick Tip**

Addition : counting forward

e.g.    5 + 7 = _____

Count 7 forward from 5.

```
    1   2   3   4   5   6   7
  5   6   7   8   9   10  11  12  13
```

5 + 7 = 12

Subtraction : counting backward

e.g.    11 – 4 = _____

Count 4 backward from 11.

```
        4   3   2   1
  6   7   8   9   10  11
```

11 – 4 = 7

⑱  6 + 6   = _____          ⑲  14 – 7   = _____

⑳  16 – 9  = _____          ㉑  15 – 8   = _____

㉒  7 + 9   = _____          ㉓  8 + 3    = _____

㉔  2 + 9   = _____          ㉕  12 – 5   = _____

## Match the expressions with the number sentences.  Then calculate.

**Examples**

Using tens may help you find the sum and the difference faster.

①  8 + 7 = 8 + 2 + 5 ← Break 7 into          ②  12 – 4 = 10 + 2 – 4 ← Break 12 into
        = 10 + 5          2 + 5.                      = 10 – 4 + 2          10 + 2.
        = 15                                          = 6 + 2
                                                      = 8

㉖

| 15 take away 8  ○ |     | ○  12 – 7  = _____ |
| 12 take away 7  ○ |     | ○  8 + 9   = _____ |
| 8 plus 9        ○ |     | ○  7 + 7   = _____ |
| 7 plus 7        ○ |     | ○  15 – 8  = _____ |
| 16 take away 8  ○ |     | ○  16 – 8  = _____ |

## Solve the problems.

㉗

Aunt Doris buys 9 red apples and 5 green apples.  How many apples does she buy in all?

_____ + _____ = _____

She buys _____ apples in all.

+
_____

㉘

6 dogs and 8 cats are in a pet shop.  How many dogs and cats are there in all?

_____ + _____ = _____

There are _____ dogs and cats in all.

+
_____

㉙

Uncle Bill has 15 muffins.  6 of them are chocolate.  How many are not chocolate?

_____ – _____ = _____

_____ muffins are not chocolate.

–
_____

㉚

Melody had 12 lollipops.  She ate 4 of them.   How many lollipops does she have now?

_____ – _____ = _____

She has _____ lollipops now.

–
_____

 **MIND BOGGLER**

### Read what Derek says.  Answer the question.

I have 11 baseball cards and  my brother has 5 baseball cards. How many cards do I need to give him so that each of us has the same number of cards?

Derek needs to give _____ baseball cards to his brother.

# 10 Measurement II

**Look at the pictures. Put a check mark ✔ in the circle to tell which takes longer to do.**

① Ⓐ eat a cookie    Ⓑ bake a cookie    ② Ⓐ wash hands    Ⓑ bathe a dog

③ Ⓐ knit a sweater    Ⓑ wear a sweater    ④ Ⓐ sing a song    Ⓑ ring a bell

**Write morning, afternoon, evening or night to tell what time of the day John does the following things.**

⑤   eats breakfast

_____

⑥   goes to bed

_____

⑦   eats dinner

_____

⑧   goes home

_____

**Write one thing you will do in the following times.**

⑨ Morning : _____    Afternoon : _____

Evening : _____    Night : _____

**See what Jeffrey will be doing this week. Help him fill in the blanks and answer the questions.**

| Sunday | Monday | Tuesday | Wednesday | Thursday | Friday | Saturday |
|--------|--------|---------|-----------|----------|--------|----------|

⑩  Jeffrey is going to the [Cinema] on _____ with his mom.

⑪  Jeffrey is going to have [Coke] for lunch on _____ .

⑫  Jeffrey is going to play [bat] on _____ .

⑬  Jeffrey goes to the [LIBRARY] to borrow some books on _____ .

⑭  _____ is the day Jeffrey has a [crayon] lesson.

⑮  On _____ , Jeffrey goes to a [cake] .

⑯  How many days are there in a week?                    _____ days

⑰  Which day comes right after Thursday?              _____

⑱  How many days will Jeffrey have [pizza] for lunch?   _____ days

⑲  How many days will Jeffrey be going to play sports?   _____ days

⑳  Jeffrey likes playing hockey. Which day of the week
     is Jeffrey's favourite day?                                    _____

㉑  After borrowing the books, Jeffrey will return them
     the next day. Which day will he return the books?    _____

## Match the months with the pictures.  Circle the correct months.

| ㉒ *[heart with flowers "Valentine's Day"]* | January / February / December | ㉓ *[Christmas tree]* | May / July / December | ㉔ *[jack-o'-lantern]* | July / September / October |
|---|---|---|---|---|---|
| ㉕ *[beach scene]* | March / July / November | ㉖ *[bare tree with falling leaves]* | February / June / October | ㉗ *[snowman in snow]* | January / August / April |

## Circle the correct answers to complete the sentences.

㉘ There are  11 / 12 / 13  months and  2 / 3 / 4  seasons in a year.

㉙ July / June / November  comes just after May.

㉚ August is in  spring / summer  and October is in  fall / winter .

㉛ Winter / Spring  is the coldest season and  fall / summer  is the hottest season.

## Look at the calendar.  Answer the questions.

### May

| Sun | Mon | Tues | Wed | Thu | Fri | Sat |
|---|---|---|---|---|---|---|
|  |  |  | 1 | 2 | 3 | 4 |
| 5 | 6 | 7 | 8 | 9 | 10 | 11 |
| 12 | 13 | 14 | 15 | 16 | 17 | 18 |
| 19 | 20 | 21 | 22 | 23 | 24 | 25 |
| 26 | 27 | 28 | 29 | 30 | 31 |  |

Quick Tip

The way to read a calendar :

first day of the month

AUGUST ← month

Aug 18, on Sunday

days of a week

last day of the month

㉜ Which month comes just after this month?  _____

㉝ Which day of the week is May 3?  _____

㉞ Which day of the week is the first day of May?  _____

㉟ Mother's day is on the 2nd Sunday.  What is the date?  _____

㊱ John's birthday is on the 3rd Wednesday.  What is the date?  _____

**Examples**

①

The long hand points to 12 and the short hand points to 4.

It is 4:00 or 4 o'clock.

②

The long hand points to 6 and the short hand points midway between 4 and 5.
It is 4:30.

## Tell the times.

③⑦

_____

③⑧

_____

③⑨

_____

④⓪

_____

④①

_____

④②

_____

## Draw the clock hands to show the times.

④③ 5 o'clock
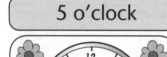

④④ 7:30

④⑤ 3:00

## MIND BOGGLER

**Put a mirror on the line to see what time the clock shows.**

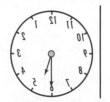

It is _____ .

# 11 3-D Figures

**Colour the figures in the pictures to match the colours given. Then count and write the numbers.**

| red | yellow | blue | green | orange | brown |
|-----|--------|------|-------|--------|-------|

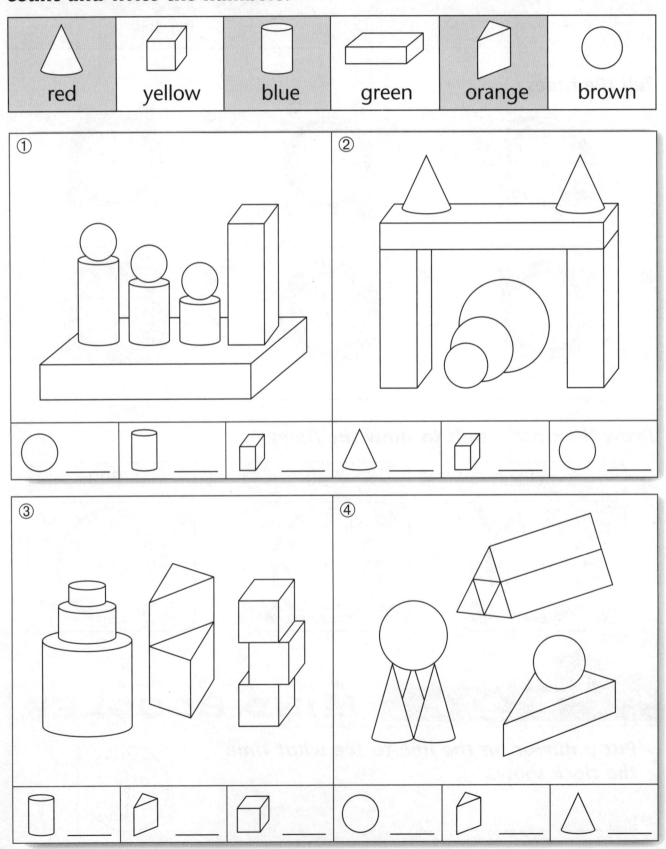

# Look at each group of solids. Cross out **X** the one that does not belong.

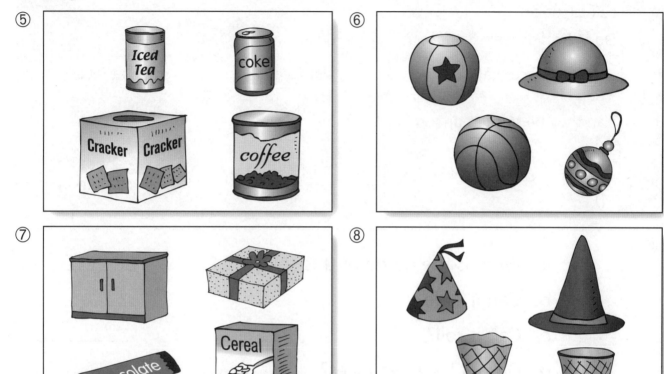

⑤

Iced
Tea

coke

Cracker    Cracker

coffee

⑥

⑦

Cereal

chocolate

⑧

# Match and write the names of the solids.

| Cylinder | Cone | Cube | Sphere | Triangular prism |

⑨

CHIPS

chocolate

_____

_____

_____

_____

_____

# Look at the figures. Answer the questions.

⑩

a. What is the name of this solid?  _____

b. Can it slide?  _____

c. Can it roll?  _____

d. Does it have flat faces?  _____

⑪

a. What is the name of this solid?  _____

b. Can it slide?  _____

c. Can it be stacked on top of another one?  _____

d. Does it have flat faces?  _____

⑫

a. What is the name of this solid?  _____

b. Can it roll?  _____

c. Can it be stacked on top of another one?  _____

d. Does it have curved faces?  _____

⑬

a. What is the name of this solid?  _____

b. Can it roll?  _____

c. Can it slide?  _____

d. Does it have curved faces?  _____

**Jimmy puts the solids in different groups. Find out his sorting rules and check ✔ the correct answers.**

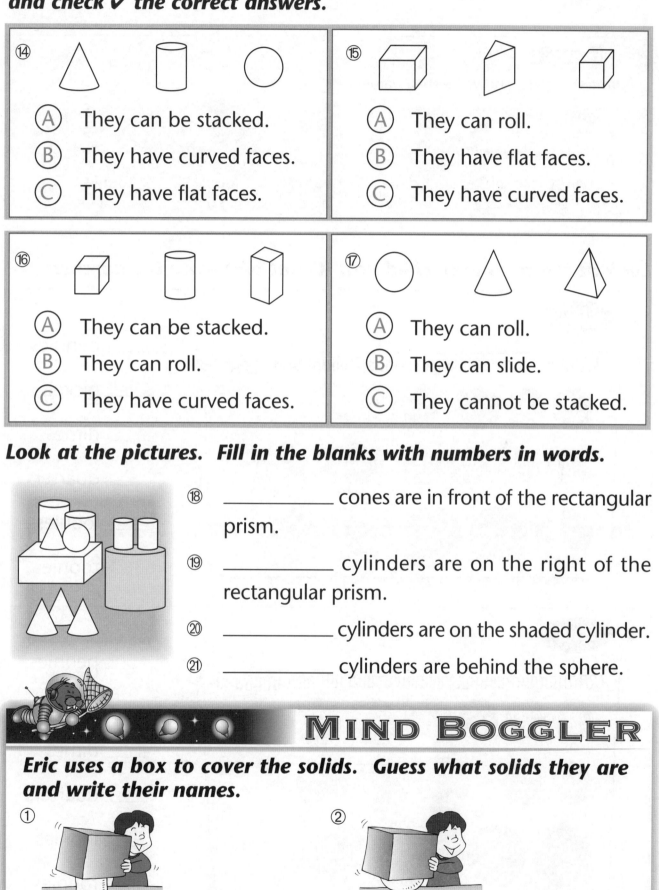

⑭

Ⓐ   They can be stacked.

Ⓑ   They have curved faces.

Ⓒ   They have flat faces.

⑮

Ⓐ   They can roll.

Ⓑ   They have flat faces.

Ⓒ   They have curved faces.

⑯

Ⓐ   They can be stacked.

Ⓑ   They can roll.

Ⓒ   They have curved faces.

⑰

Ⓐ   They can roll.

Ⓑ   They can slide.

Ⓒ   They cannot be stacked.

**Look at the pictures. Fill in the blanks with numbers in words.**

⑱   _____ cones are in front of the rectangular prism.

⑲   _____ cylinders are on the right of the rectangular prism.

⑳   _____ cylinders are on the shaded cylinder.

㉑   _____ cylinders are behind the sphere.

# MIND BOGGLER

**Eric uses a box to cover the solids. Guess what solids they are and write their names.**

①   _____

②   _____

# 12 Money

### Example

Name the coins and write their values.

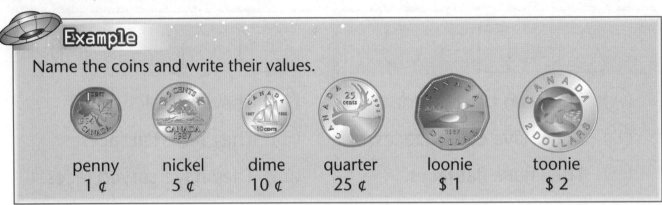

| penny | nickel | dime | quarter | loonie | toonie |
|-------|--------|------|---------|--------|--------|
| 1 ¢ | 5 ¢ | 10 ¢ | 25 ¢ | $ 1 | $ 2 |

## Look at the coins each child has.  Count and write the numbers.

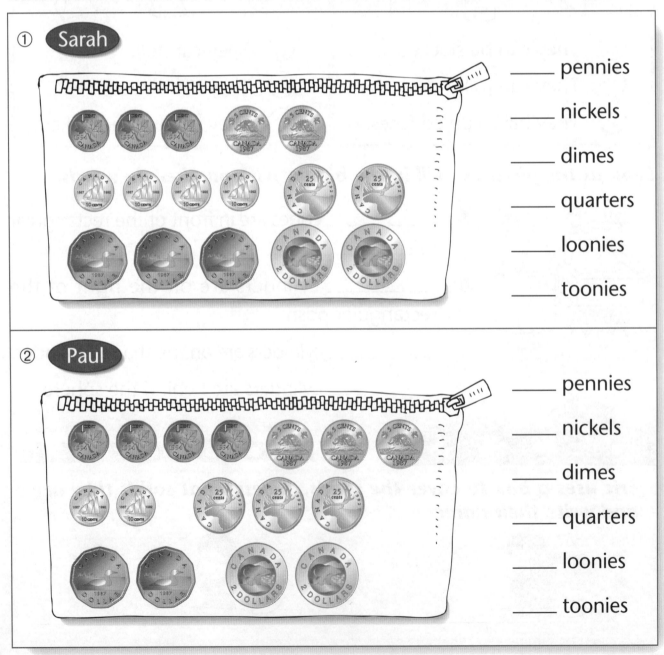

① **Sarah**

_____ pennies

_____ nickels

_____ dimes

_____ quarters

_____ loonies

_____ toonies

② **Paul**

_____ pennies

_____ nickels

_____ dimes

_____ quarters

_____ loonies

_____ toonies

## Check ✔ the coins in each group to match the value on the left.

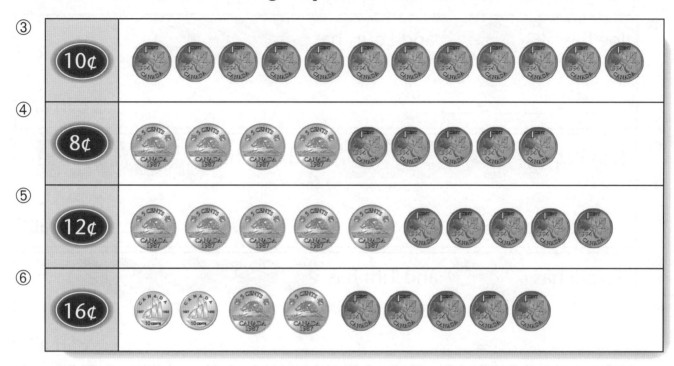

## See how much money each child has. Write the amount and answer the questions.

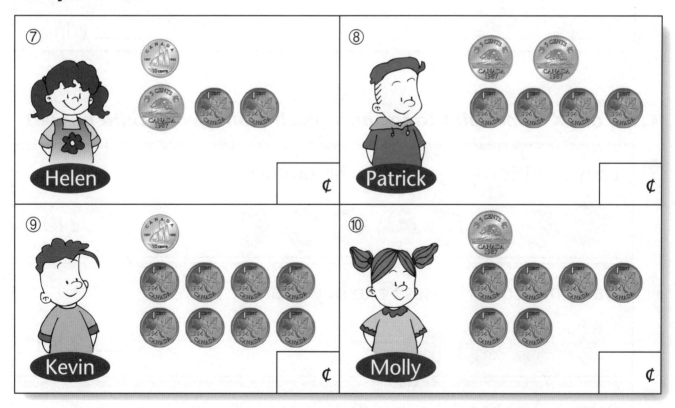

⑪  Which child has the fewest coins?  _____

⑫  Which child has the most money?  _____

## Find how much money the children have in all.

⑬ Joe has  and Louis has  .

_____ + _____ = _____            _____ ¢ in all

⑭ Ken has  and Rick has  .

_____ + _____ = _____            _____ ¢ in all

⑮ Teresa has  and Tim has  .

_____ + _____ = _____            _____ ¢ in all

⑯ Mandy has  and Cindy has  .

_____ + _____ = _____            _____ ¢ in all

## Cross out ✗ some coins to see how much money each child has left.

⑰ Larry has 12¢.  He gives 8¢ to his brother.

             _____ ¢ left

⑱ David has 16¢.  He uses 5¢ to buy a candy.

          _____ ¢ left

⑲ Rebecca has 14¢.  She uses 6¢ to buy a lollipop.

           _____ ¢ left

## *See what the children are going to buy.  Help them solve the problems.*

⑳ a.       b.  Sally has

\_\_\_\_\_ + \_\_\_\_\_ = \_\_\_\_\_     \_\_\_\_\_ – \_\_\_\_\_ = \_\_\_\_\_

They cost \_\_\_\_\_ ¢.     She has \_\_\_\_\_ ¢ left.

㉑ a.       b.  Robert has

\_\_\_\_\_ + \_\_\_\_\_ = \_\_\_\_\_     \_\_\_\_\_ – \_\_\_\_\_ = \_\_\_\_\_

They cost \_\_\_\_\_ ¢.     He has \_\_\_\_\_ ¢ left.

㉒ a.       b.  Linda has

\_\_\_\_\_ + \_\_\_\_\_ = \_\_\_\_\_     \_\_\_\_\_ – \_\_\_\_\_ = \_\_\_\_\_

They cost \_\_\_\_\_ ¢.     She has \_\_\_\_\_ ¢ left.

 **MIND BOGGLER**

*Edward had a*  *.  He bought 3 different items from the above and has*  *left.  Colour the 3 items he bought.*

Ⓐ   Ⓑ   Ⓒ   Ⓓ   Ⓔ

57

# 13 Graphs

Mrs. Murdoch asked her Grade 1 students their favourite pets. Look at the graph and answer the questions.

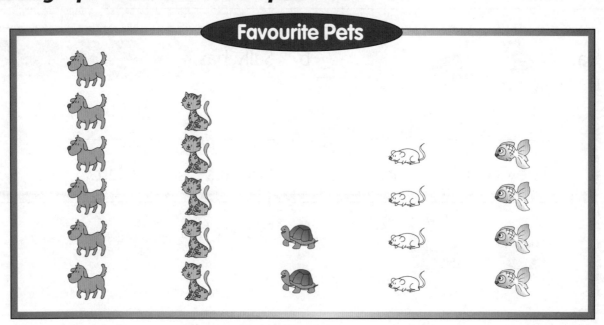

Favourite Pets

① How many students like  best?          _____ students

② How many students like  best?          _____ students

③ How many students like best?          _____ students

④ How many more students like
than ? ?          _____ more students

⑤ How many students are there in
Mrs. Minden's class?          _____ students

⑥ Which pet is the least popular?  Colour it.

⑦ Which pet is the most popular?  Colour it.

**Mr. White asked the children their favourite movies. Look at the graph and answer the questions.**

⑧ How many  like  ? _____

⑨ How many  like  ? _____

⑩ How many children like  ? _____ children

⑪ How many more children like  than
 ? _____ more children

⑫ How many  are there? _____

⑬ How many  are there? _____

⑭ How many children are there? _____ children

⑮ Colour the most popular movie blue and the least one yellow.

**Count the toys Tim has and write the numbers. Then colour the graph to show his toys and answer the questions.**

⑯

a. 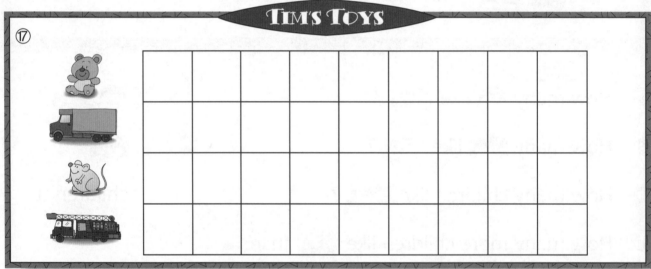 _____    b. _____ _____

c. _____ _____    d. _____ _____

**Quick Tip**

To count accurately, cross out ✘ each toy as you are counting it.

⑰

### TIM'S TOYS

⑱ How many toy cars does Tim have?    _____ toy cars

⑲ How many toy animals does Tim have?    _____ toy animals

⑳ How many more 🐻 than 🐭 does Tim have?    _____ more

㉑ How many toys does Tim have in all?    _____ toys

㉒ 5 🚚 are yellow.  How many 🚚 are not yellow?    _____ 🚚

60

**Each child in Ms. Gibbon's class drew his or her favourite fast food on the board.  Colour the graph to show their preferences and circle the correct answers.**

### Our Favourite Fast Foods

㉓

㉔  How many children are in Ms. Gibbon's class?            21    22    23

㉕  How many children like 🌭 best?                              2     6     7

㉖  How many children like 🍕 best?                              5     6     7

㉗  Which fast food do most children like?

## MIND BOGGLER

**Look at the graph above.  Answer the questions.**

①  How many kinds of fast foods do the children like?

_____ kinds

②  Ms. Gibbon wants to buy one kind of fast food to treat her students.  What should she buy?  Give the reason.

_____

# 14 Probability

**Decide if the following are likely or unlikely to occur. Circle 'Yes' or 'No'.**

**Look at the picture stories.  Circle 'Yes' if they are likely to happen or 'No' if they are not.**

**Each child can spin the arrow once and gets the food that the arrow lands on. Read and help the children check ✔ the correct spinners.**

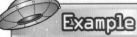

**Example**

Which spinner has a greater chance for getting 'fries'?

A

B

Spinner A has a greater chance for getting fries.

⑯ Shirley likes sandwiches. Which spinner should she choose?

Ⓐ

Ⓑ

Ⓒ

⑰ Leon likes pizzas. Which spinner should he choose?

Ⓐ
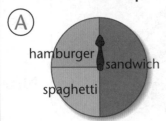

Ⓑ

Ⓒ

⑱ Eva doesn't like hamburgers. Which spinner should she choose?

Ⓐ

Ⓑ

Ⓒ

⑲ Louis chooses a spinner that will never get pita. Which spinner does he choose?

Ⓐ

Ⓑ

Ⓒ

**Use the words given to describe the chances.**

never          sometimes          often

⑳ Matthew is going to pick a ball from a box with 5 balls.

a. The chance of picking a  _____

b. The chance of picking a  _____

c. The chance of picking a  _____

㉑ Elaine shuffles 4 cards for Matthew to pick.

a. The chance of picking a | **1** | _____

b. The chance of picking a | **2** | _____

c. The chance of picking a | **3** | _____

㉒ Matthew is going to spin.

a. The chance of getting a  _____

b. The chance of getting a  _____

c. The chance of getting a  _____

# MIND BOGGLER

**Read what Matthew says.  Give a reason to tell why he is wrong.**

There are 5 red balls and 2 yellow balls inside the box.  I have a greater chance of picking a red ball.

_____

_____

**Find out how many shapes will cover each picture.  Answer the questions.**

①

    a.  What shape is the shaded part?

        _____

    b.  How many ▮ are needed to cover the picture?

        _____ ▮

②

    a.  What shape is the shaded part?

        _____

    b.  How many ◢ are needed to cover the picture?

        _____ ◢

**Joyce coloured one face of each solid.  Help her answer the questions.**

③

    a.  What is the name of the solid?      _____

    b.  What is the shape of the shaded face?      _____

④

    a.  What is the shape of the shaded face?      _____

    b.  What is the shape of the spotted face?      _____

⑤

    a.  What is the name of the solid?      _____

    b.  What is the shape of the shaded face?      _____

## *Extend the patterns.*

⑥  A  B  B  C  A  B  B  C  A  B  B  C  ___  ___  ___  ___

⑦  4  4  2  2  1  4  4  2  2  1  4  4  ___  ___  ___  ___

⑧  △  △  ◯  ▼  △  △  ◯  ▼  △  △  ___  ___  ___  ___

⑨  1  3  2  1  1  3  2  1  1  3  2  1  ___  ___  ___  ___

## *Circle 'Yes' or 'No' to show if the following are likely or unlikely to happen.*

| ⑩ | Snow in winter | Yes | No |
|---|---|---|---|
| ⑪ | School in September | Yes | No |
| ⑫ | Swimming in a lake in January | Yes | No |
| ⑬ | Ice-skating on a lake in July | Yes | No |
| ⑭ | Butterflies flying in the sea | Yes | No |
| ⑮ | Going to see a movie on Monday | Yes | No |

## *Jane wants to share her snacks with her brother.  Help her divide the snacks into 2 equal halves with a line.*

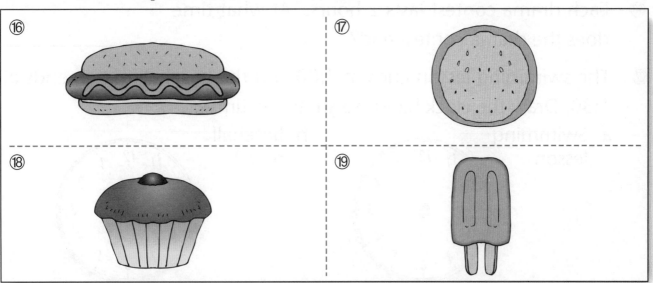

⑯  ⑰  ⑱  ⑲

**Look at Melody's calendar. Answer the questions and solve the problems.**

Swimming lesson **Start**

Baseball match **Start** `12:00`

Drama contest **Start** `01:30`

| March | | | | | | |
|---|---|---|---|---|---|---|
| Sunday | Monday | Tuesday | Wednesday | Thursday | Friday | Saturday |
|  |  | 1 | 2 | 3 | 4 | 5 |
| 6 | 7 | 8 | 9 | 10 | 11 | 12 |
| 13 | 14 | 15 | 16 | 17 | 18 | 19 |
| 20 | 21 | 22 | 23 | 24 | 25 | 26 |
| 27 | 28 | 29 | 30 | 31 |  |  |

⑳ How many days are there in a week? _____

㉑ Which month comes just after this month? _____

㉒ Which day of a week is March 15? _____

㉓ Melody has a swimming lesson in March. What is the date? _____

㉔ Melody has a baseball match in March. At what time does the match start? _____

㉕ How many days will the drama contest be held? What are the dates? _____

㉖ Each drama contest lasts 2 hours. At what time does the drama contest end? _____

㉗ The swimming lesson ends at 3:00 and the baseball match ends at 1:30. Draw the clock hands to show the times.

    a. Swimming lesson

    b. Baseball match

## Add or subtract.

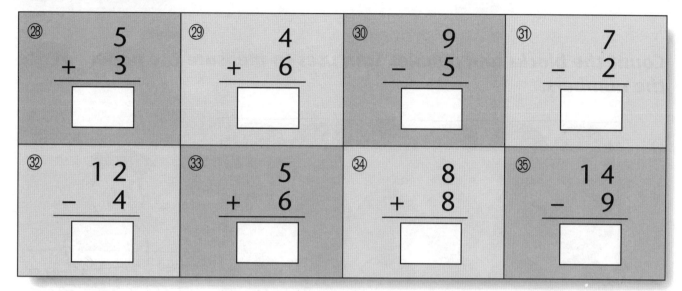

㊲ 10 – 8 = _____     ㊲ 3 + 6 = _____

㊳ 5 + 9 = _____     ㊴ 11 – 8 = _____

㊵ 9 + 9 = _____     ㊶ 16 – 7 = _____

## Solve the problems.

㊷ There are 15 fish in the fish tank.  Aunt Sabrina takes away 6 fish. How many fish are left in the fish tank?

_____ ◯ _____ = _____          _____ fish

㊸ Tim has 8 stamps.   Uncle Bill gives Tim 5 more.  How many stamps does Tim have in all?

_____ ◯ _____ = _____          _____ stamps in all

㊹ Ray has 9 storybooks in French and 6 storybooks in English.  How many storybooks does Ray have in all?

_____ ◯ _____ = _____          _____ storybooks in all

㊺ Aunt Mary has 11 hamburgers.  She gives 2 hamburgers to her son. How many hamburgers are left?

_____ ◯ _____ = _____          _____ hamburgers

**Count the blocks and pennies Sam uses to measure the paper. Write the numbers.**

㊻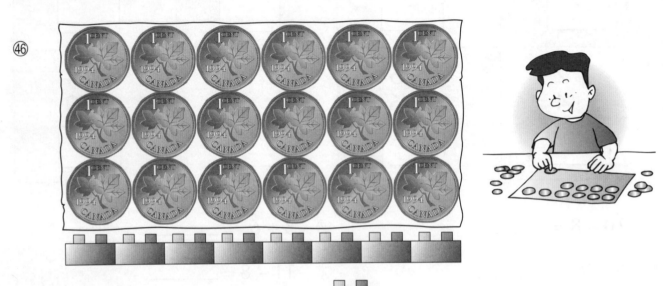

a.   The paper is as long as _____ ⬚ .

b.   _____ pennies are needed to cover the paper.

**Count by 2's, 5's or 10's to find the number of hairpins in each group. Then answer the questions.**

㊼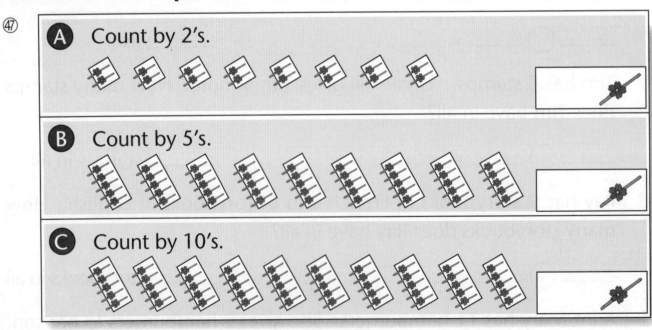

A   Count by 2's.

B   Count by 5's.

C   Count by 10's.

㊽   Which group has the most hairpins?          Group _____

㊾   Which group has the least hairpins?          Group _____

## Look at the prices of the treats.  Solve the problems.

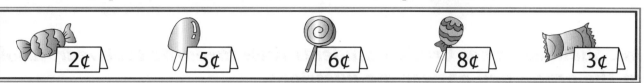

50  Check ✔ the coins to show the values of the treats.

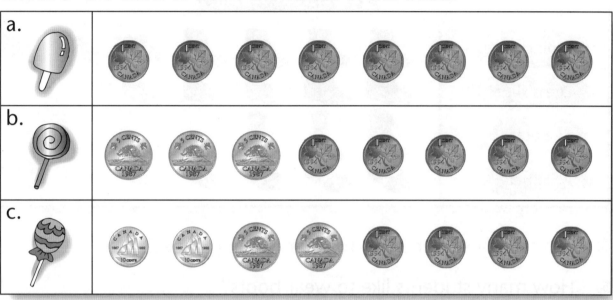

51  Sally wants to buy a 🍬 and a 🍭.  How much does she need to pay?

_____ + _____ = _____                    _____ ¢

52  Ray wants to buy a 🍭 and a 🍭.  How much does he need to pay?

_____ + _____ = _____                    _____ ¢

53  Sarah had 10¢.  She bought a 🍬.  How much does she have now?

_____ – _____ = _____                    _____ ¢

54  Tom had 15¢.  He bought a 🍭.  How much does he have now?

_____ – _____ = _____                    _____ ¢

55  Peter bought a 🍭 and had 5¢ left.  How much had he got at first?

_____ + _____ = _____                    _____ ¢

**Ms. Shim asked her Grade 1 students their favourite footwear. Look at the graph and answer the questions.**

**Favourite Footwear**

Running shoes

Dress shoes

Boots

Slippers

■ Boys
■ Girls

56  How many students like to wear running shoes? _____

57  How many students like to wear boots? _____

58  How many boys like to wear slippers? _____

59  How many girls like to wear dress shoes? _____

60  How many more students like to wear running shoes than boots? _____

61  How many students like to wear dress shoes and slippers? _____

62  Which is the most popular footwear? _____

63  Which is the least popular footwear? _____

64  Today all the children wear their favourite shoes except those who like slippers. The boys who like slippers wear running shoes and the girls who like slippers wear dress shoes.

   a.  How many students wear running shoes? _____

   b.  How many students wear dress shoes? _____

## Review

1. 8 ; eight
2. 1 ; one
3. 4 ; four
4. 5 ; five
5. Alex ; Paul
6. 5th ; 8th
7. 8
8.
9.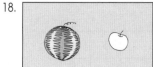
10.

11. 3 ; 5 ; 6
12. 6 ; 7 ; 9
13. 5 ; 8 ; 10
14. inside
15. in front of
16. above
17. on

18.

19.

20.

21.

22.

23.

24. B , A , C
25. A , B , C

26.

27.

28.

29.

30.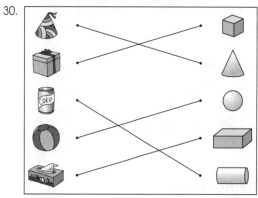

31.
green    yellow    red    blue

32.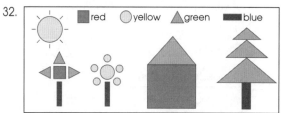
red   yellow   green   blue

## 1   Numbers 1 - 20

1a. 16 ; ✔
b. 15
2a. 9
b. 11 ; ✔
3a. 13 ; ✔
b. 12
4a. 18 ; ✔
b. 17
5. 10
6. 12
7. 7
8. 8
9. 11
10. 8
11. Thirteen
12. eighteen
13. Eighteen
14. two
15. one

16.
17.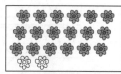

18.
19.

20.
21.

22.     23.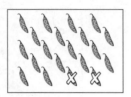

24. 12 ; 5 ; 7        25. 10 ; 4 ; 6
26. 11 ; 8 ; 3        27. 10 ; 11
28. 1

## Mind Boggler

■ = red apples   ▦ = green apples
□ = golden apples

9

## 2 Sequencing

1. 1 ; 3 ; 2 ; 4        2. 2 ; 1 ; 4 ; 3
3. 4 ; 1 ; 2 ; 3        4. 1 ; 4 ; 2 ; 3
5. 3 ; 1 ; 2 ; 4
6.         7.
8. 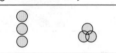        9.

10.-12. (Suggested answers)
10.

11.

12.

13.

14.

15. 

16.     17.     18.

19.     20. 

21. 10 ; 12 ; 18        22. 11 ; 10 ; 7
23. 13 ; 4              24. 2 ; 3
25. 10 ; 8 ; 7          26. 9 ; 10 ; 10

### Mind Boggler

## 3 Addition

1. 7        2. 6
3. 8        4. 9
5. 8        6. 4
7. 6        8. 6
9. 8        10. 5
11. 9       12. 8
13. 7       14. 6
15. 10      16. 10
17. 10      18. 9
19. 8

20.

| + | 1 | 2 | 3 | 4 | 5 |
|---|---|---|---|---|---|
| 1 | 2 | 3 | 4 | 5 | 6 |
| 2 | 3 | 4 | 5 | 6 | 7 |
| 3 | 4 | 5 | 6 | 7 | 8 |
| 4 | 5 | 6 | 7 | 8 | 9 |
| 5 | 6 | 7 | 8 | 9 | 10 |

21.  2      22.  4      23.  5
   + 5        + 3        + 4
   ———        ———        ———
     7          7          9

24.  3      25.  2
   + 3        + 6
   ———        ———
     6          8

26. 4 + 2 = 6        27. 3 + 1 = 4
28. 6 + 3 = 9        29. 7 + 2 = 9
30. 1 + 4 = 5        31. 5 + 5 = 10
32. 4 ; 3 ; 7    33. 5 ; 4 ; 9    34. 6 ; 4 ; 10
      4              5              6
    + 3            + 4            + 4
    ———            ———            ———
      7              9             10

35. Ann        36. Andy

### Mind Boggler

George

## 4 Subtraction

1. 6 ; 6

2. 4 ; 4    

3. 1 ; 1    

4. 5 ; 5    

5. 8 ; 8

6. 3 ; 3

7.   8
   − 3
   ——
     5

8.   6
   − 5
   ——
     1

9.   7
   − 4
   ——
     3

10.   5
    − 2
    ——
      3

11.   4
    − 3
    ——
      1

12. 6 ; 4          13. 4 ; 5
14. 5             15. 3
16. 3             17. 2
18. 6             19. 1
20. 8             21. 2
22. 3             23. 7
24. 4             25. 4
26. 7 − 2 = 5     27. 6 − 2 = 4
28. 4 − 1 = 3     29. 7 − 6 = 1
30. 9 − 4 = 5
31. 3             32. 3
33. 7             34. 3
35. 2             36. 2
37. 6             38. 6

## Mind Boggler

4

## 5   Measurement I

1.      2.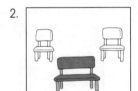

3.      4.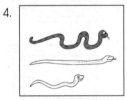

5. 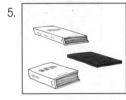     6.

7. 7 ; 4          8. 11 ; 6
9. 10 ; 6         10. 5 ; 3
11. 9 ; 5
12a. 3 ; 2        b. 7 ; 4
13. B             14. A
15. C
16.-18. (Individual answers)
19. (Suggested answers)
    10 ; 6 ; 6 ; 9

## Mind Boggler

12

## 6   Patterns

1. ✔             2. ✔
3. ✗             4. ✗
5. 3 ; ◆ ▲ ▲     6. 4 ; ★ ★ ♥ ♥
7. 3 ; ● ■ ●     8. 3 ; ▌▌ ▬
9. 4 ; ▲ ● ● ●
10. ○ × ○        11. **4  6  3**
12. **T  P  G**   13. ○ ○ ∘
14. △ ▲ ▽

15. - 18. ( △ yellow  ○ red  □ blue  ▯ green  ⬡ purple )

15. △ ○ ○ □ △ ○ ○ □
16. ▯ ○ ⬡ ▯ ○ ○ ▯ ○
17. ▯ □ □ △ ▯ □ □ △
18. ⬡ ○ □ ▯ □ ○ ○ □

19a. 10 ; 9 ; 8 ; 7
  b.
  c. down ; 1
20a. 1 ; 2 ; 3 ; 4
  b.
  c. triangles ; 1
21. 6 ; 7 ; 8          22. 8 ; 7 ; 6
23.
24.
25.
26a.-c.  ▨ = green   ■ = blue
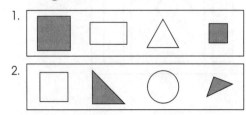

  d. Yes

## Mind Boggler

1. pattern ; shape      2. size ; shape

## 7   2-D Figures

1.
2.

3.
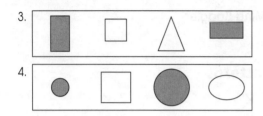

4.

5. A 6. B
7. A 8. B
9. triangles ; 3 10. rectanlges ; 4
11. circles ; 6 12. squares ; 5
13. Yes 14. No
15. Yes 16. No
17. No 18. Yes
19.

20.

21. 22.

23. 24.

25. ✔ 26. ✔
27. ✗ 28. ✗
29. ✔ 30. ✗
31. ✔ 32. ✗
33.
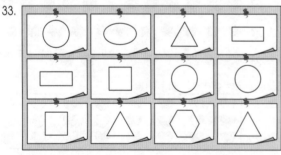

34. 3 35. 2

## Mind Boggler
(Suggested answers)
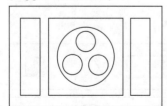

## Progress Test
1a. 8 b. 5 c. 13 d. 3
2a. 6 b. 9 c. 15 d. 3
3. 12 4. 10
5. fork 6. 2
7. 1 ; 3 ; 2 ; 4 8. 4 ; 2 ; 1 ; 3
9. 3 + 4 = 7 10. 6 + 3 = 9
11. 8 – 5 = 3 12. 7 – 2 = 5
13. 9 14. 3
15. 4 16. 6
17. 4 18. 9
19. 4 20. 3
21. 24 22. 20
23. A 24. C
25a. b. triangles
26a. b. squares
27a. b. circles

28. 7 ; 2 ; 7 + 2 = 9 ; 9
29. 9 ; 9 – 7 = 2 ; 2
30. 4 ; 4 ; 4 + 4 = 8 ; 8
31. 10 ; 10 – 9 = 1 ; 1
32. 8 ; 8 – 5 = 3 ; 3

## 8 Numbers to 100
1. - 4. (Estimate: Individual answers)
1. 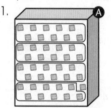 A 41 2. 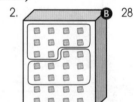 B 28
3. 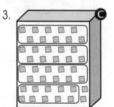 C 42 4. 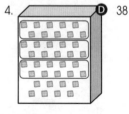 D 38

5. C 6. 1
7. 10 8. 40
9. Lucy 10. Janice
11. Alex 12. Lucy
13. Nancy 14. Lucy
15. Brenda 16. No
17. 42 ; 40 ; 35 ; 25 ; 19 18. 20 ; 41 ; 65 ; 70 ; 82
19a. 5 ; 7 b. 57
20a. 4 ; 9 b. 49
21a. 6 ; 4 b. 64
22. 36 23. 75
24. 64 25. 65

26.-28.

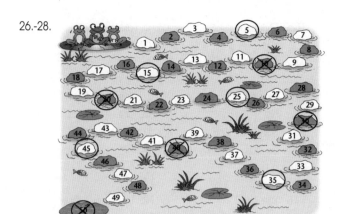

## Mind Boggler

1. No

2. No

3. 10, 20, 30, 40, 50

4. 10, 20, 30, 40, 50

## 9  Addition and Subtraction

1. 14 ; 14
2. 6 + 7 = 13 ; 13
3. 8 + 4 = 12 ; 12
4. 5 + 8 = 13 ; 13
5. 6 + 9 = 15 ; 15
6. 8 + 8 = 16 ; 16
7. 5 ; 9 ; 9
8.

16 – 7 = 9 ; 9

9.

15 – 7 = 8 ; 8

10.

12 – 9 = 3 ; 3

11.

13 – 8 = 5 ; 5

| | |
|---|---|
| 12. 8 | 13. 17 |
| 14. 9 | 15. 15 |
| 16. 2 | 17. 13 |
| 18. 12 | 19. 7 |
| 20. 7 | 21. 7 |
| 22. 16 | 23. 11 |
| 24. 11 | 25. 7 |

26.

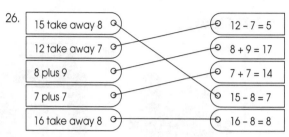

27. 9 + 5 = 14 ; 14

$$\begin{array}{r} 9 \\ + \ 5 \\ \hline 14 \end{array}$$

28. 6 + 8 = 14 ; 14

$$\begin{array}{r} 6 \\ + \ 8 \\ \hline 14 \end{array}$$

29. 15 – 6 = 9 ; 9

$$\begin{array}{r} 15 \\ - \ 6 \\ \hline 9 \end{array}$$

30. 12 – 4 = 8 ; 8

$$\begin{array}{r} 12 \\ - \ 4 \\ \hline 8 \end{array}$$

## Mind Boggler

3

## 10 Measurement II

| | |
|---|---|
| 1. B | 2. B |
| 3. A | 4. A |
| 5. morning | 6. night |
| 7. evening | 8. afternoon |
| 9. (Individual answers) | |
| 10. Friday | 11. Saturday |
| 12. Saturday | 13. Monday |
| 14. Thursday | 15. Tuesday |
| 16. 7 | 17. Friday |
| 18. 2 | 19. 3 |
| 20. Wednesday | 21. Tuesday |
| 22. February | 23. December |
| 24. October | 25. July |
| 26. October | 27. January |
| 28. 12 ; 4 | 29. June |
| 30. summer ; fall | 31. Winter ; summer |
| 32. June | 33. Friday |
| 34. Wednesday | 35. May 12 |
| 36. May 15 | |
| 37. 7 o'clock / 7:00 | 38. 9:30 |
| 39. 2 o'clock / 2:00 | 40. 12 o'clock / 12:00 |
| 41. 11:30 | 42. 8:30 |

43.       44.      45.

## Mind Boggler

5:30

## 11 3-D Figures

1.
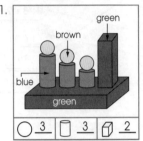

2.
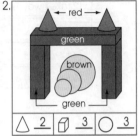

3.
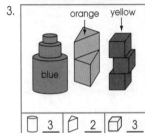

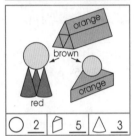

5.

6.

7.

8.

9.
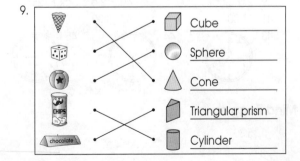

10a. Cylinder    b. Yes
  c. Yes    d. Yes
11a. Cube    b. Yes
  c. Yes    d. Yes
12a. Cone    b. Yes
  c. No    d. Yes
13a. Sphere    b. Yes
  c. No    d. Yes
14. B    15. B
16. A    17. C
18. Three    19. Three
20. Two    21. Two

### Mind Boggler

1. Cylinder    2. Sphere

## 12 Money

1. 3 ; 2 ; 4 ; 2 ; 3 ; 2    2. 4 ; 3 ; 2 ; 3 ; 2 ; 2

3.

4.

5.

6.

7. 17    8. 14
19. 18    10. 11
11. Helen    12. Kevin
13. 7 + 8 = 15 ; 15    14. 6 + 9 = 15 ; 15
15. 6 + 7 = 13 ; 13    16. 8 + 5 = 13 ; 13

17.

4

18. 11

19. 8

20a. 5 + 8 = 13 ; 13    b. 14 – 13 = 1 ; 1
21a. 7 + 6 = 13 ; 13    b. 16 – 13 = 3 ; 3
22a. 4 + 8 = 12 ; 12    b. 15 – 12 = 3 ; 3

### Mind Boggler

A ; B ; E

## 13 Graphs

1. 6    2. 5
3. 4    4. 2
5. 21    6. 🐢
7. 🐕    8. 4
9. 6    10. 6

11. 3
12. 10
13. 12
14. 22
15. ↳blue   ↳yellow

16a. 5   b. 9
   c. 3   d. 4

17.
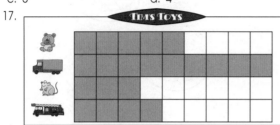

18. 13   19. 8
20. 2   21. 21
22. 4

23.
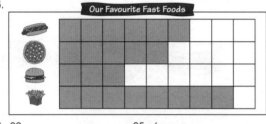

24. 22   25. 6
26. 5   27.

## Mind Boggler

1. 4
2. She should buy fries. A lot of students like fries.

# 14 Probability

1. Yes   2. No
3. Yes   4. No
5. No   6. Yes
7. Yes   8. No
9. No   10. Yes
11. Yes   12. No
13. Yes   14. Yes
15. No   16. A
17. C   18. C
19. A   20a. Often
   b. Sometimes   c. Never
21a. Never   b. Sometimes
   c. Often   22a. Sometimes
   b. Often   c. Never

## Mind Boggler

The yellow balls are bigger than the red balls, so there is a greater chance to pick a yellow ball than a red ball.

# Final Test

1a. rectangle   b. 44
2a. triangle   b. 40
3a. Cube   b. Square
4a. Triangle   b. Rectangle
5a. Cylinder   b. Circle
6. A B B C   7. 2 2 1 4
8. ○ ▼ △ △   9. 1 3 2 1
10. Yes   11. Yes
12. No   13. No
14. No   15. Yes

16.

17.
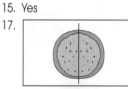

18.
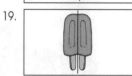
19.

20. 7   21. April
22. Tuesday   23. March 7
24. 12:00
25. 2 days ; March 10 and March 24
26. 3:30

27a.    b.

28. 8   29. 10
30. 4   31. 5
32. 8   33. 11
34. 16   35. 5
36. 2   37. 9
38. 14   39. 3
40. 18   41. 9
42. 15 – 6 = 9 ; 9   43. 8 + 5 = 13 ; 13
44. 9 + 6 = 15 ; 15   45. 11 – 2 = 9 ; 9
46a. 8   b. 18
47. A 16 ; B 45 ; C 50
48. C   49. A

50a.
b.
c.

51. 2 + 8 = 10 ; 10   52. 6 + 8 = 14 ; 14
53. 10 – 3 = 7 ; 7   54. 15 – 8 = 7 ; 7
55. 6 + 5 = 11 ; 11
56. 7   57. 3

58. 3
60. 4
62. Running shoes
64a. 10

59. 3
61. 11
63. Boots
b. 8

## Game Cards

A.
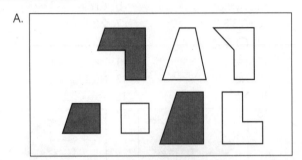

B.

A dinosaur

C.
 = 3
 = 2
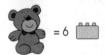 = 6

6 blocks

D.
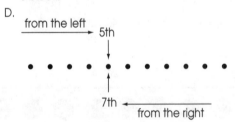

There are 11 houses.

E.
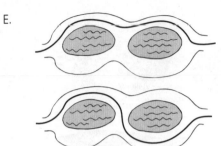

4 routes

F.
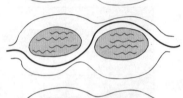